KITCHEN
TABLE

100 Fish and Seafood Recipes

KITCHEN TABLE gives you a wealth of recipes from your favourite chefs. Whether you want a quick weekday supper, sumptuous weekend feast or food for friends and family, let Rick, Ken, Madhur, Antonio, Ainsley, Mary and Annabel bring their expertise to your table.

For exclusive recipes, our regular newsletter, blog and news about Apps for your phone, visit www.mykitchentable.co.uk

Throughout this book, when you see visit our site for practical videos, tips and hints from the My Kitchen Table team.

KITCHEN
TABLE

100 Fish and
Seafood Recipes
RICK STEIN

Welcome to  KITCHEN TABLE

I've selected **100 of my most easy-to-follow recipes** for this book. Many take inspiration from my travels around the world, but there are also plenty of favourites from past menus in Padstow and dishes that I think really celebrate some of the fresh produce that can be found around the British coast today.

Rick Stein

Contents

Classic Fish Soup with Rouille and Croûtons

I've always thought that a good fish soup is the best way to test the quality of a good fish restaurant. It's all to do with the depth of flavour that comes from using lots of fish and shellfish with saffron, tomatoes, red peppers, fennel, garlic and, always for me, orange peel.

Step one To make the rouille, cover the bread with the fish stock or water and leave to soften. Squeeze out the excess liquid and put the bread into a food processor with the harissa, garlic, egg yolk and ¼ teaspoon of salt. Blend until smooth. With the machine still running, gradually add the oil until you have a smooth, thick mayonnaise-like mixture.

Step two Fillet the fish, removing any bones. Heat the olive oil in a large pan, add the vegetables and garlic and cook gently for 20 minutes, or until soft but not coloured. Add the orange zest, tomatoes, red pepper, bay leaf, thyme, saffron, prawns, cayenne pepper and fish fillets.

Step three Cook briskly for 2–3 minutes, then add the fish stock and orange juice, bring to the boil and simmer for 40 minutes. Meanwhile, make the croûtons (see below).

Step four Liquidise the soup and pass through a sieve into a clean pan, pressing out as much liquid as possible with the back of a ladle. Return the soup to the heat and season to taste with the cayenne, salt and pepper.

Step five Ladle the soup into a warmed tureen and put the croûtons, Parmesan cheese and rouille into separate dishes. To serve, ladle the soup into warmed bowls and leave each person to spread some rouille onto the croûtons, float them on their soup and sprinkle them with some of the Parmesan.

To make croûtons, thinly slice 1 baguette then fry the slices in olive oil until crisp and golden. Drain on kitchen paper and then rub a garlic clove over one side of each piece.

Serves 4

for the rouille

25g (¼ oz) day-old white bread

a little fish stock or water

2 tbsp good-quality harissa

2 garlic cloves

1 egg yolk

250ml (9fl oz) olive oil

for the soup

900g (2lb) mixed fish, such as gurnard, dogfish, cod and grey mullet

85ml (3fl oz) olive oil

75g (3oz) each onion, celery, leek and fennel, chopped

3 garlic cloves, sliced

juice of ½ orange, plus 2 pared strips of orange zest

200g (7oz) tinned chopped tomatoes

1 small red pepper, deseeded and sliced

1 bay leaf

sprig of thyme

pinch of saffron strands

100g (4oz) unpeeled, cooked North Atlantic prawns

pinch of cayenne pepper

1.2 litres (2 pints) good-quality fish stock

25g (1oz) Parmesan, finely grated, to serve

Sardines Stuffed with Pine Nuts, Currants, Capers, Parsley and Orange Zest

This seems to me to be the perfect recipe for sardines. Best eaten cold, ideally a day later, they are well worth the effort required to make them.

Serves 7 as part of a mixed mezze

14 large (or 20 small sardines)

14–20 fresh bay leaves

1 orange, halved lengthways, then sliced

for the stuffing

50g (2oz) currants

4 tbsp extra-virgin olive oil, plus extra for drizzling

1 onion, finely chopped

4 garlic cloves, finely chopped

pinch of crushed dried chillies

75g (3oz) fresh white breadcrumbs

2 tbsp freshly chopped flat-leaf parsley

15g (½oz) anchovy fillets in olive oil, drained and chopped

2 tbsp small capers, chopped

zest of ½ small orange, plus 1 tbsp orange juice

25g (1oz) finely grated Pecorino or Parmesan

50g (2oz) pine nuts, lightly toasted

Step one To prepare the sardines, rub off the scales and rinse the fish under cold running water. Cut the head off the fish and discard, then slit open along the belly, down to the tail, and pull out the guts. Wash the cavities clean, then open up each fish and place belly-side down on a chopping board. Press firmly along the backbone until the fish lies completely flat, then turn it over and pull away the backbone, snipping it off close to the tail. Remove any bones left behind with fish tweezers and then season lightly with salt.

Step two Preheat the oven to 200°C/400°F/gas 6 and oil a shallow 20x30cm (8x12in) baking dish. For the stuffing, cover the currants in hot water and set them aside for 10 minutes to plump up. Heat the oil in a frying pan, add the onion, garlic and crushed dried chillies, and cook gently for 6–7 minutes until the onion is soft but not browned. Take the pan off the heat and stir in the breadcrumbs, parsley, anchovies, capers, orange zest and juice, cheese and pine nuts. Drain the currants well and stir in, then season to taste with salt and pepper.

Step three Spoon about 1½ tablespoons of the stuffing (depending on the size of the fish) along the head end of each sardine and roll them up towards the tail. Pack them tightly into the oiled shallow baking dish, arranging them with their tails pointing upwards, and place a bay leaf and a half slice of orange between each one.

Step four Season the fish lightly with salt and pepper, drizzle over a little more oil and bake for 20 minutes. Serve at room temperature, or cold as part of an assortment of antipasti.

Crab and Sweetcorn Soup

This is the first oriental dish I ever ate at a Chinese restaurant, in Peterborough, England, in 1964, and it is a world classic that is so often ruined by sickly sweet tins of creamed corn, tasteless crab and gloopy cornflour. I thought it would be interesting to restore the dish to its simplicity and reliance on good, fresh ingredients.

Step one Bring the chicken stock to the boil in a pan. Meanwhile, stand the corn cobs up on a board and slice away the kernels with a large sharp knife. Add the corn to the stock and simmer for 5 minutes.

Step two Check over the crabmeat for any little pieces of shell, keeping the meat in the largest pieces possible. Mix the cornflour to a smooth paste with a little cold water, stir it into the soup and simmer for 2 minutes.

Step three Stir in the crabmeat, ginger, spring onions, soy sauce, rice wine or sherry, 1 teaspoon of salt and some pepper to taste. Simmer for 1 minute.

Step four Now give the soup a good stir, remove the spoon and slowly trickle in the beaten egg white so that it forms long, thin strands in the soup. Simmer for about 30 seconds and then serve immediately.

Serves 4

1.2 litres (2 pints) good-quality chicken stock

2 fresh corn cobs

225g (8oz) fresh white crabmeat

5 tsp cornflour

1 tsp very finely chopped fresh root ginger

2 spring onions, cut into 2½ cm (1in) pieces and finely shredded lengthways

1 tbsp light soy sauce

1 tbsp Chinese rice wine or dry sherry

1 egg white, lightly beaten

Hot and Sour Fish Soup

You can use any fillets of small fish or shellfish for this recipe, such as lemon sole, plaice, flounder, prawns, scallops and even cooked mussels dropped in at the end and heated through.

Serves 4

4 red bird's eye chillies, chopped

2½ cm (1in) piece of fresh galangal or root ginger, chopped

1 tsp blachan (dried shrimp paste)

3 garlic cloves, chopped

6 shallots, chopped

½ tsp light muscovado sugar

3–4 tbsp tamarind water or lemon juice

100g (4oz) squid (pouches and tentacles)

1 litre (1¾ pints) chicken stock

3 tbsp Thai fish sauce

75g (3oz) snake beans or French beans, cut into small pieces

100g (4oz) monkfish fillet, cut into slices

150g (5oz) baby pak choy, cut into 2½ cm (1in) pieces, or 50g (2oz) baby leaf spinach

to garnish

a small handful of coriander leaves

1 red chilli, deseeded and sliced

Step one Put the chillies, galangal or ginger, blachan, garlic, shallots and sugar into a mortar or a food-processor and work to a coarse paste, adding a little of the tamarind water, or lemon juice, if necessary.

Step two Cut the body pouch of the squid open along one side and score the inner side with the tip of a small, sharp knife into a fine diamond pattern. Cut the squid into approximately 3cm (1¼in) squares and cut the tentacles into bite-size pieces.

Step three Bring the chicken stock and the rest of the tamarind water, or lemon juice, to the boil in a pan. Add the spice paste and simmer for 10 minutes. Strain through a muslin-lined or very fine sieve and add the Thai fish sauce and the beans. Simmer for 1 minute. Add the monkfish and squid and simmer for 1 minute. Add the pak choy or spinach and simmer for a further minute. Ladle the soup into warmed bowls and serve sprinkled with the coriander leaves and red chilli.

To make tamarind water, take a piece of tamarind pulp the size of a tangerine and put in a bowl with 150ml (5fl oz) warm water. Work the paste into the water with your fingers until it has broken down and all the seeds have been released. Strain the liquid. Keep the tamarind water in the fridge for up to 24 hours.

Cod and Lobster Chowder

I can't resist slipping a chowder or two into each of my books – I love that subtle combination of salt pork, seafood and cream. Try this with clams, mussels and any flaky white fish.

Step one First remove the meat from the cooked lobster. Put the lobster belly side down onto a board and ensure none of the legs are tucked underneath. Cut it in half lengthways, first through the middle of the head between the eyes. Then turn either the knife or the lobster around and finish cutting it in half through the tail. Open it up and lift out the tail meat from each half. Remove the intestinal tract from the tail meat. Break off the claws and then break them into pieces at the joints. Crack the shells with a knife. Remove the meat from each of the claw sections in as large pieces as possible. Remove the soft greenish tomalley (liver) and any red roe from the head of the shell with a teaspoon and set aside. Pull out the stomach sac and discard.

Step two Put two of the water biscuits into a plastic bag and crush to very fine crumbs with a rolling pin. Then mix with the tomalley, other soft material from the head and half the butter; or blend everything in a small food-processor.

Step three Cut the piece of salt pork or bacon into small dice. Heat the rest of the butter in a medium-sized pan, add the pork or bacon and fry over a medium heat until lightly golden. Add the onion and cook gently until softened. Stir in the flour and cook for 1 minute. Gradually stir in the milk, then add the potatoes and bay leaf and simmer for 10 minutes or until the potatoes are just tender. Add the cod and simmer for 4–5 minutes. Lift the fish out of the milk and break the flesh into large flakes with a wooden spoon.

Step four Stir in the water-biscuit paste, lobster meat and cream and simmer for 1 minute. Season with the cayenne pepper, 1 teaspoon of salt and some black pepper. To serve, coarsely crush the two remaining biscuits and sprinkle them over the soup along with the chopped parsley.

Serves 4

450–550 g (1–1¼ lb) lobster, freshly cooked

4 water biscuits

50g (2oz) butter, softened

100g (4oz) salt pork or rindless streaky bacon, in one piece

1 small onion, finely chopped

15g (½ oz) plain flour

1.2 litres (2 pints) milk

2 potatoes (about 225g/8oz), peeled and diced

1 bay leaf

450g (1lb) thick cod fillet, skinned

120ml (4fl oz) double cream

pinch of cayenne pepper

2 tbsp freshly chopped parsley, to garnish

Skate with Tomato, Saffron, Garlic and Sultanas

This dish is so easy to do, and it's something really quite special. In Cabra, Italy, they served it at room temperature as an antipasto along with some other dishes, but it's equally good served warm.

Serves 4

2 x 225g (8oz) skinned and trimmed skate wings

for the sauce

100ml (3½ fl oz) extra-virgin olive oil

6 garlic cloves, finely chopped

1 x 400g tin good-quality plum tomatoes

30g (1¼ oz) sultanas

pinch of saffron strands

pinch of crushed dried chillies

2 fresh bay leaves

1 tsp caster sugar

1 tsp small capers, drained and rinsed, to serve

Step one First make the sauce. Put the olive oil and garlic into a medium-sized pan. Place over a medium heat and as soon as the garlic begins to sizzle, add the tomatoes, sultanas, saffron, dried chillies, bay leaves, sugar and ½ teaspoon salt. Bring up to a gentle simmer and leave to cook for 30 minutes, stirring every now and then and breaking up the tomatoes with a wooden spoon. Remove the bay leaves, season to taste with salt and pepper and keep warm.

Step two Bring 1.5 litres (2½ pints) water to the boil in a large shallow pan. Add 1 tablespoon of salt and the skate wings and leave them to simmer gently for 10 minutes until cooked.

Step three Lift the skate wings out of the water onto a board and cut each one into two or three pieces. Spoon slightly more than half the tomato sauce onto the base of a warmed oval serving dish and place the pieces of skate on top. Spoon the rest of the sauce down the centre of the skate, scatter with the capers and serve.

Spiced Octopus Salad with Parsley

I've been slow-cooking octopus and cuttlefish in olive oil with aromatic herbs and spices for some time, and this recipe was inspired by the spicing of a lot of dishes in the Mediterranean region, especially Corfu.

Step one Preheat the oven to 110°C/225°F/gas ¼. To clean the octopus, turn the body pouch inside out and pull away the entrails and bone-like strips sticking to the sides. Locate the stomach sac, which is about the size of an avocado stone, and cut it away. Wash the octopus well inside and out and then turn the body right-side out again. Press out the beak and the soft surround from the centre of the tentacles, cut out and discard.

Step two Put the octopus into a small casserole with the olive oil, cinnamon, cloves, allspice berries, peppercorns and 1 teaspoon of salt. Cover with a tight-fitting lid and bake for 2 hours or until tender.

Step three Remove the casserole from the oven and lift the octopus onto a plate. Strain the cooking juices into a small pan and boil rapidly until reduced by about half and really well flavoured. Leave to cool along with the octopus.

Step four When the octopus is cool, cut off the tentacles and slice each one across on the diagonal into slices about 5mm (¼in) thick. Cut the body into similar-sized pieces.

Step five Put the octopus in a bowl and stir in 3 tablespoons of the reduced cooking liquor, the lemon juice and the parsley. Toss together well, spoon into a shallow serving dish and drizzle with the extra-virgin olive oil just before serving at room temperature.

Serves 4 as a starter or 8 as part of a mixed mezze

1 octopus, weighing about 750g–1kg (1lb 10oz–2lb 4oz)

50ml (2fl oz) extra-virgin olive oil

7.5cm (3in) piece cinnamon stick

4 cloves

6 allspice berries

1 tsp black peppercorns

to finish

¾ tsp fresh lemon juice

1 tbsp coarsely chopped flat-leaf parsley

2 tsp extra-virgin olive oil

Oyster Soup with Ginger, Soy and Chilli

This soup really celebrates the subtle flavours of oysters. For perfect results, the stock that you use needs to be chilled until the fat sets on the top and can be strained off, otherwise there will always be disappointing droplets on the top of your otherwise beautifully clear soup.

Serves 4

12 Pacific oysters

1.5 litres (2½ pints) cold good-quality chicken stock

2 tsp Thai fish sauce

1 tsp light soy sauce

1 medium-hot green chilli, deseeded and roughly chopped

1cm (½ in) piece of fresh root ginger, sliced

100g (4oz) cheap white fish fillet, finely chopped

50g (2oz) leeks, thinly sliced

1 egg white

a few leaves of tarragon, chervil and young flat-leaf parsley, to garnish

Step one Open the oysters and pour off the juices into a bowl. Release the oyster meats from their shells and keep them chilled until needed.

Step two Put the oyster juice, cold chicken stock, Thai fish sauce, soy sauce, green chilli, ginger, chopped fish, leeks, egg white and 1 teaspoon of salt into a large pan. Place over a medium heat and slowly bring to the boil, giving the mixture a stir every now and then. Allow the stock to vigorously boil for 5–10 seconds, then reduce the heat and leave it to simmer undisturbed for 30 minutes.

Step three Pass the soup into a clean pan through a fine sieve lined with a double thickness of muslin. Slice the oyster meats lengthways into 2 or 3 slices, depending on their size. Bring the soup back to the boil, add the oyster slices and leave them to cook gently for just 5 seconds. Then ladle the soup into warmed bowls and scatter each one generously with the herb leaves. Serve immediately.

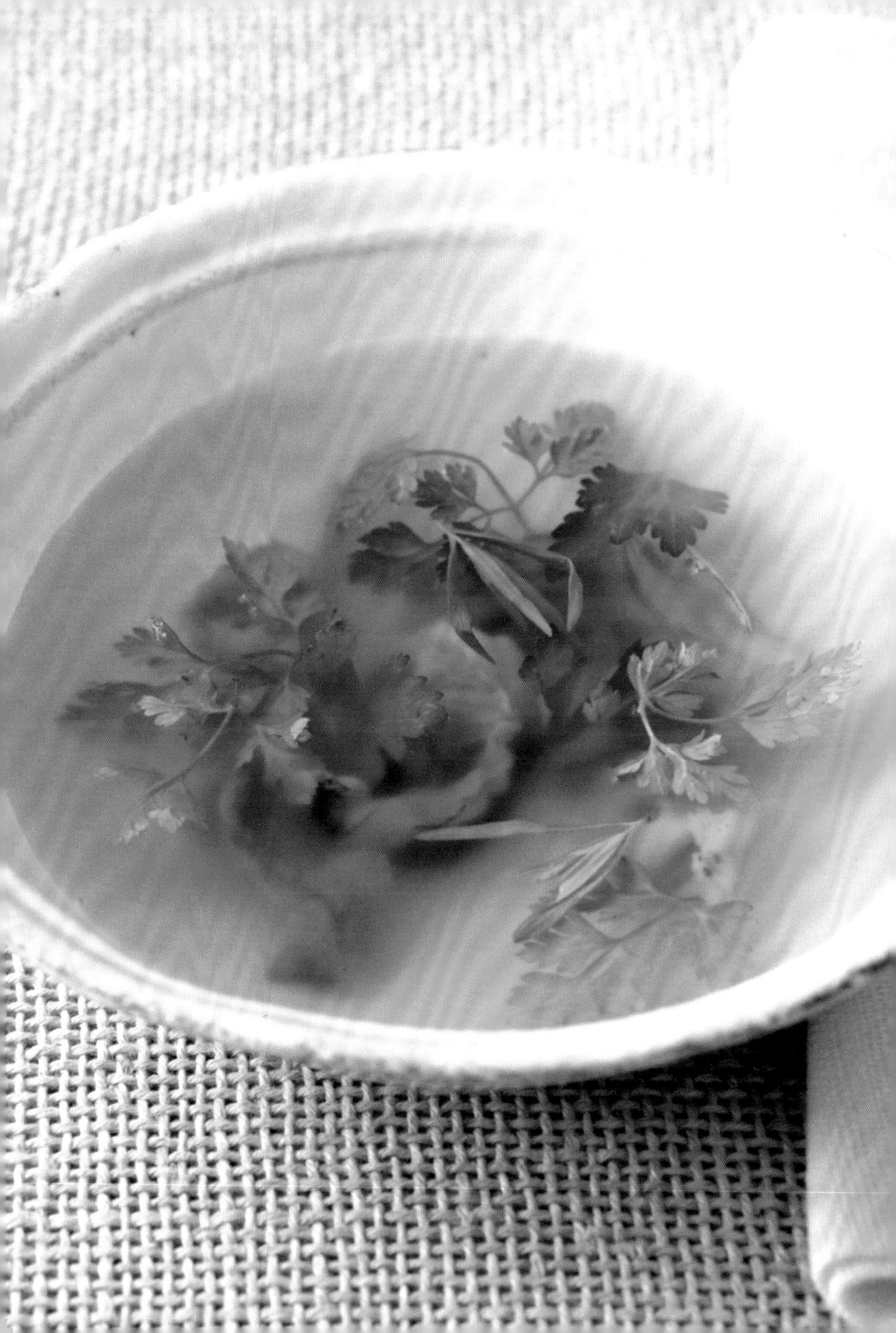

Seafood Tempura

This is the recipe from the Japanese ambassador's residence in London where we filmed his chefs. The two most important tips I picked up were firstly to make the batter at the very last minute and hardly whisk it at all, and secondly to fry everything in small batches.

Step one Mix together the ingredients for each dipping sauce and divide between two shallow dipping saucers or bowls.

Step two Clean the squid pouches inside and out then cut across into thin rings, and separate the tentacles into pairs. Remove the heads from the prawns and then peel them, leaving the last tail segment in place. Cut the lemon sole fillets diagonally across into strips about the thickness of your little finger.

Step three Heat some oil for deep-frying to 190°C/375°F or until a cube of day-old bread rises to the surface and browns in about a minute. To make the batter, sift half the flour, half the cornflour and a pinch of salt into a large bowl, and sift the remaining flour and cornflour and a pinch of salt into another. Just before you start cooking, stir half the ice-cold soda water into one lot of flour/cornflour until only just mixed; the batter should still be a little bit lumpy and, if it seems a bit thick, add a drop more water. When it's cooked, you want it to coat the food in a very thin, almost transparent layer.

Step four Drop eight pieces of mixed seafood into the batter, lift out one at a time and drop immediately into the hot oil. Fry for just 1 minute until crisp and lightly golden, then lift out and drain on lots of kitchen paper. Repeat with the remaining seafood, using the second bowl of batter when the first is used up, then transfer to a warmed platter, together with a bowl of each dipping sauce, and eat immediately while still crisp and hot.

Serves 8

250g (9oz) squid (pouches and tentacles)

20 raw tiger prawns

250g (9oz) skinned lemon sole fillet

lots of sunflower oil, for deep-frying

for the tempura batter

115g (4¼ oz) plain flour

115g (4¼ oz) cornflour

300ml (¼ pint) ice-cold soda water, from a new bottle

sea salt

for the soy and ginger dipping sauce

90ml (3fl oz) dark soy sauce

2 thin slices of peeled fresh root ginger, very finely chopped

½ bunch of thin spring onions, very thinly sliced

for the sweet chilli dipping sauce

150ml (5fl oz) sweet chilli sauce

1 tbsp light soy sauce

¼ tsp Chinese five-spice powder

1½ tbsp cold water

Sea Bream with a Sauce Vierge of Baby Fennel, Spring Onions, Tomato and Mint

This dish comes from a really attractive seafood restaurant, Le Pirate, in the fishing village of Erbalunga, just outside Bastia on Corsica.

Serves 4

4 heads baby fennel

1 x 450g (1lb) gilt-head bream, cleaned and trimmed

8 tbsp extra-virgin olive oil, plus extra for brushing

2 tbsp fresh lemon juice

4 cherry tomatoes, quartered

2 thin spring onions, trimmed and thinly sliced

2 garlic cloves, thinly sliced

½ medium-hot red chilli, deseeded and thinly sliced across

6 mint leaves, finely shredded

Step one Preheat the grill to high. Trim the baby fennel down to 15cm (6in) and then cut each one in half lengthways. Drop them into a pan of boiling, lightly salted water and blanch for 1½ minutes until al dente. Drain and refresh under cold running water. Drain well on kitchen paper.

Step two Brush the fish on both sides with a little olive oil, season with salt and pepper and place on an oiled baking tray or the rack of the grill pan. Cook for 10 minutes, turning it over halfway through. Meanwhile, put the oil, lemon juice, tomatoes, spring onions, garlic, chilli, ½ teaspoon of salt and 10 turns of the black pepper mill into a small pan. Set aside.

Step three Lift the fish onto a chopping board. Using a small, sharp knife, cut through the skin all around the outside edge of the fish, across the base of the tail and behind the gills, and pull it away. Run your knife down the length of the fish between the two top fillets, and ease them apart and away from the underlying bones. Slide a palette knife under each of the fillets in turn and carefully lift them away. Set them aside on a warmed plate. Now, lift up the backbone of the fish by the tail and carefully ease it away from the bottom fillets, taking the head with it, and discard. Slice down the centre of the bottom fillets and clean away any bones and skin from the outside edges. Lift the bottom fillets away from the skin and add them to the plate.

Step four Add the pieces of blanched fennel to the pan of sauce vierge and place it over a low heat. Warm through gently for 1 minute. First lift out the fennel and overlap two pieces in the centre of each warmed serving plate. Put one fish fillet on top. Stir the mint leaves into the remaining sauce, spoon a little over the fish and fennel and serve immediately.

Squid Fried in Olive Oil with Smoked Pimentón and Garlic Mayonnaise

Dust the squid in a coarse flour to give a nice crisp texture. In Spain, the country this recipe originates from, there is a flour specially milled for frying – harina de trigo; fine-ground semolina is the closest we can get to it here.

Step one To make the smoked pimentón and garlic mayonnaise, put the garlic cloves onto a chopping board, sprinkle with a large pinch of salt and crush into a smooth paste with the flat side of the blade of a large knife. Stir into the mayonnaise along with the smoked pimentón and a little more salt to taste, and set aside for a few minutes to allow the flavours time to develop.

Step two Cut the squid pouches across into thin rings and separate the tentacles into pairs. Spread the rings and tentacles out onto a tray and season lightly with salt and pepper.

Step three Pour olive oil into a large, deep frying pan to a depth of 1cm (½in) and heat to 190°C/375°F over a medium-high heat. Toss the squid in the harina de trigo, semolina or flour, knock off the excess and leave for 1–2 minutes so that the flour becomes slightly damp. This will give it a crisper finish.

Step four Shallow-fry the squid in small batches for 1 minute until crisp and lightly golden. Drain briefly on kitchen paper, transfer to a warmed serving dish and repeat with the remaining squid. Serve hot, with the smoked pimentón and garlic mayonnaise and lemon wedges.

Serves 4 as a starter or 8 as part of a mixed mezze

250g (9oz) cleaned squid (pouches and tentacles)

olive oil, for shallow-frying

harina de trigo, fine-ground semolina or plain flour, for dusting

lemon wedges, to serve

for the smoked pimentón and garlic mayonnaise

2 garlic cloves

200g (7oz) mayonnaise (see page 39)

1 tsp smoked pimentón (Spanish paprika)

Cream of Mussel Soup with Celeriac and Saffron

I always like to add a few mussels in the shell along with the rest of the mussel meats to improve the finished look. It's important to get the texture of the soup right before adding them, which is why I pass it first through a normal sieve then through an even finer sieve, called a chinois. And finally, I can't stress strongly enough to reheat the mussels with extreme caution. The longer they cook, the more they lose their flavour of the sea.

Serves 4

750g (1lb 10oz) small mussels, cleaned

4 tbsp dry white wine

50g (2oz) butter

225g (8oz) peeled celeriac, chopped

125g (4½ oz) leek, sliced

1 small garlic clove, chopped

about 750ml (1¼ pints) good-quality fish stock

good pinch of saffron strands

175g (6oz) vine-ripened tomatoes, roughly chopped

4 tbsp crème fraîche

Step one Put the mussels and 2 tablespoons of the wine into a medium-sized pan. Place over a high heat and cook for 2–3 minutes or until the mussels have just opened. Tip them into a colander set over a bowl to collect the cooking juices, and discard any mussels that have not opened. Leave to cool slightly then remove the meats from three-quarters of the shells, cover and set aside.

Step two Melt the butter in a clean pan, add the celeriac, leek, garlic and remaining wine. Cover and cook gently for 5 minutes.

Step three Put all but the last tablespoon or two of the mussel liquor (which might be a bit gritty) into a large measuring jug and make up to 900ml (1½ pints) with the fish stock. Add to the pan of vegetables along with the saffron and tomatoes, cover and simmer gently for 30 minutes.

Step four Leave the soup to cool slightly, then blend until smooth. First pass through a sieve, then pass once more through a chinois into a clean pan, bring back to the boil. Stir in the crème fraîche and some seasoning to taste.

Step five Remove the pan from the heat and stir in the mussels to warm them through briefly, but don't allow them to cook any more than they already have. Ladle the soup into warmed soup plates, trying to distribute the mussels evenly, and serve immediately.

Spider Crab Soup with Fennel, Tomato and Pernod

The meat of the spider crab is wonderfully fragrant and sweet. The whole point of this soup is to sum up the seafood flavours of Provence.

Step one First, remove the white meat from the crab. Place the crab, back-shell down, on a chopping board and lift up the tail flap, break off and discard. Twist off all the legs, break them at the joints and discard all but the first, largest joints. Crack the shells of the legs with the back of a knife or a hammer and hook out the white meat with a crab pick. To remove the white meat from the body section, insert the blade of a large knife between the body and the back shell and twist to release it. Remove and reserve about 1 tablespoon of the brown meat from the back shell and discard the rest. Pull off the feathery gills or 'dead man's fingers' from the body and discard. Using a large knife, cut the body section into four and pick out the white meat from the little channels with a crab pick.

Step two Clean and trim the leek and fennel. To make a stock, put the pieces of crab shell, the leek and fennel trimmings, the tablespoon of brown meat and the vegetable stock into a large pan. Bring slowly up to the boil, skimming off any scum as it rises to the surface, cover and simmer for 30 minutes.

Step three Meanwhile, cut the leek lengthways into quarters, then across into pieces the size of a small fingernail. Cut the fennel and deseeded tomatoes into similar-sized pieces.

Step four Warm the olive oil in a pan, add the dried chilli, fennel seeds, orange peel, tomato purée, garlic, leek and fennel and cook gently for 5 minutes without letting it colour. Increase the heat a little, add the pastis and light it with a match to burn off the alcohol. Strain in the stock through a fine sieve, add the orange juice and saffron and simmer for 10 minutes. Now add the crabmeat and tomato and season to taste with salt and pepper. Ladle into warmed soup plates and serve immediately.

Serves 4–6

1 x 500g (1lb) cooked spider or brown crab

1 leek

1 head fennel

1.2 litres (2 pints) vegetable stock

2 tomatoes (about 175g/6oz), skinned and deseeded

4 tbsp olive oil

small pinch of crushed dried chillies

pinch of fennel seeds, lightly crushed

1 pared strip of orange peel

½ tsp tomato purée

4 garlic cloves, sliced

50ml (2fl oz) pastis, such as Pernod or Ricard

juice of ½ an orange

pinch of saffron strands

Prawn Dumpling and Noodle Soup with Chilli, Mint and Coriander

This is a typically clear, light, Vietnamese-style soup with noodles, dumplings and some thinly sliced salad vegetables.

Serves 4

for the soup

3.5 litres (6 pints) good-quality chicken stock

8 garlic cloves, sliced

5cm (2in) piece root ginger, peeled and sliced

3 tbsp Thai fish sauce

160g (5¾oz) thin Asian-style noodles

1 medium-hot red chilli, thinly sliced

4 tsp lime juice

30g (1¼oz) spring onions, sliced

125g (4½oz) fresh beansprouts

small handful of fresh mint and coriander leaves

for the dumplings

240g (8½oz) lean minced pork

2g pinch of Thai shrimp paste

1 egg

80g (3oz) peeled raw prawns

Step one Put the stock into a large pan along with the garlic, ginger and fish sauce. Leave to simmer for 1 hour. Strain into a clean pan and continue to simmer until reduced to 1.2 litres (2 pints). Keep hot.

Step two To make the dumplings, put the minced pork into a food-processor with the shrimp paste, egg and ¼ teaspoon salt and process into a smooth paste. Slice the prawns lengthways, remove the black, thread-like vein, and then slice them across into small pieces. Transfer the minced pork paste to a bowl and stir in the chopped prawns. Shape 10–15g (¼–½oz) pieces of the mixture into small balls and place on an opened-out petal steamer.

Step three Heat four deep soup bowls in a low oven. Fill a large shallow pan with water to a depth of 2cm (¾in) and bring to the boil. Add the petal steamer of dumplings, reduce the heat to a simmer, cover and steam for 4 minutes, or until cooked through.

Step four Divide the noodles, chilli, lime juice, spring onions, beansprouts, mint and coriander leaves between the heated bowls and top with the dumplings. Bring the stock back to the boil, pour into each bowl and serve immediately.

Salt Cod Fritters with Parsley and Garlic

This recipe comes from an excellent book, *Catalan Cuisine*. The author Coleman Andrews is the editor of *Saveur* magazine, which I have found enormously influential since its appearance in 1994. Serve with allioli.

Step one Rinse any excess salt off the cod, then put into a bowl and cover with cold water. Leave to soak in the fridge for 36–48 hours, changing the water 3–4 times a day. After this time, taste a small piece, and, if it still seems too salty, soak it for a bit longer. When it's ready, drain and cut the cod into slightly smaller pieces.

Step two Put the fish into a pan with the bay leaf and cover with fresh cold water. Bring to just below boiling point then remove the pan from the heat and leave to stand for 10 minutes. Remove the cod from the water and leave to cool, reserving the water. When the fish has cooled, remove the skin and any bones and flake the flesh.

Step three Put the potatoes into the pan of salt cod cooking water, bring to the boil and cook for 10 minutes until tender. Drain. In another pan, bring 300ml (½ pint) water and the olive oil to the boil, remove from the heat and beat in the flour to form a batter. Leave to cool slightly, then beat in the eggs, one at a time.

Step four Mash the potatoes then mix in the salt cod, garlic and parsley. Add salt and pepper to taste. Then mix the salt cod mixture into the batter. Cook over a low heat for about 10 minutes, stirring constantly, until the mixture thickens and will hold its shape when formed into balls. Leave to cool slightly.

Step five Heat some oil for deep-frying to 190°C/375°F. Form the salt cod mixture into 20 small balls using a spoon, and fry in batches, about 5–6 at a time, for 3 minutes or until a deep golden brown. Drain on kitchen paper and serve very hot.

To make allioli, crush 4 garlic cloves and work into a paste with ½ teaspoon of salt. Scrape into a bowl and add 1 egg yolk. Whisk together, then very gradually whisk in 175ml extra-virgin olive oil to make a thick mayonnaise-like mixture.

Serves 6

500g (1lb) dried salt cod fillets (bacallà/bacalao)

1 fresh bay leaf

2 medium-sized floury potatoes (about 200g/7oz each), peeled and thinly sliced

2 tbsp olive oil

50g (2oz) plain flour

3 eggs

2 garlic cloves, crushed

leaves from 2 large sprigs flat-leaf parsley, chopped

oil, for deep-frying

Razor Clams a la Plancha

You may find razor clams a little hard to get hold of, but this works equally well with small clams and indeed mussels. With large razors, slice the meats into three before serving.

Serves 4

24 razor clams, washed

good-quality extra-virgin olive oil

lemon wedges, freshly chopped parsley leaves, sea salt flakes and freshly ground black pepper, to serve

Step one Heat your largest heavy-based frying pan or a flat griddle over a high heat until very hot. Add a little olive oil and a single layer of the clams, hinge-side down.

Step two As soon as they have opened right up, turn them over so that the meats come into contact with the base of the pan, and cook for about 1 minute, until lightly browned.

Step three Turn the clams back over, drizzle over a little more olive oil and put them on a warmed serving plate. Serve with a lemon wedge or two and sprinkled with chopped parsley, a little sea salt and freshly ground black pepper and any juices from the pan. Repeat the process with any remaining clams.

Lightly Curried Crab Mayonnaise with Lamb's Lettuce

The French are very fond of adding a whisper of curry powder to delicate crab and other shellfish. It enhances the flavour perfectly.

Step one Skin the tomatoes by plunging them into boiling water for about 20 seconds. As soon as the skins split, remove and cover with cold water to stop them cooking any further. Peel off the skins and cut each tomato into thin slices, discarding the top and bottom.

Step two Put the mayonnaise into a bowl and stir in the curry powder, lemon juice and Tabasco sauce. Fold this mixture lightly through the crabmeat and season to taste with a little salt.

Step three Overlap a few slices of tomato into the centre of four small plates and season them lightly with salt. Spoon some of the crab mayonnaise on top. Toss the lamb's lettuce with the olive oil and a small pinch of salt and pile alongside. Serve with some wholemeal bread.

To make 300ml mayonnaise, put 2 egg yolks into a mixing bowl with 2 teaspoons of white wine vinegar and ½ teaspoon of salt. Rest the bowl on a cloth to stop it slipping, then lightly whisk to break the egg yolks. Use a wire whisk to beat in 300ml olive or sunflower oil, adding the oil a few drops at a time until you have incorporated it all. Alternatively, put a whole egg, the vinegar and salt into a food processor. Turn on the machine and slowly add the oil until you have a thick emulsion.

Serves 4

3–4 medium-sized vine-ripened tomatoes

5 tbsp mayonnaise

½ tsp mild curry powder

½ tsp fresh lemon juice

2 dashes Tabasco sauce

500g (1lb) fresh white crabmeat

50g (2oz) lamb's lettuce, roots trimmed

2 tsp extra-virgin olive oil

fresh wholemeal bread, to serve

Oysters with Sauce Mignonette

The first time I ever ate oysters was at Port St Louis, served with this flavoured vinegar.

Serves 2

12 oysters

for the sauce mignonette

3 tbsp good-quality white wine vinegar

1 tsp sunflower oil

¼ tsp coarsely crushed white peppercorns

1 tbsp very thinly sliced spring onion tops

Step one To open the oysters, wrap one hand in a tea towel and hold the oyster in it with the flat shell uppermost. Push the point of an oyster knife into the hinge, located at the narrowest point, and wiggle the knife back and forth until the hinge breaks and you can slide the knife between the two shells. Twist the point of the knife upwards to lever up the top shell, cut through the ligament and lift off the shell. Release the oyster meat from the bottom shell and remove, picking out any little bits of shell.

Step two Mix together the ingredients for the sauce just before serving. Put the oyster meats back into the shells and spoon a little of the sauce onto each one and serve.

Chilled Shellfish with Creamy Aïoli and Parsley Sauce

Beauduc is a smudge on the map somewhere between the Mediterranean coast of France and a network of étangs, the saltwater lagoons that are part of the Rhône delta. But there's a restaurant there called Chez Jou Jou, which is any seafood lover's dream: tellines (very small clams) with aïoli as a starter, then loup de mer (sea bass) as the main course – I don't know if there was any other choice, and I don't care really – all washed down with copious quantities of ice-cold Picpoul de Pinet. Jack Nicholson's been there, Dustin Hoffman's been there, and now me!

Step one Scrub all the shellfish with a stiff brush and pull out the beards protruding from between the shells of the mussels. Discard any that won't close when given a sharp tap on the work surface.

Step two Put the shellfish into a large pan with the wine, cover and cook over a high heat, shaking the pan every now and then, for 2–3 minutes or until they have all just opened. Tip them into a colander set over a bowl to collect the cooking juices.

Step three Return 3 tablespoons of the cooking liquid to the cooled pan with the aïoli and whisk briefly until smooth. Return the shellfish to the sauce with the prawns and 2 tablespooons of the parsley. Stir together well and leave to go cold but do not chill.

Step four To serve, spoon the shellfish onto a large oval platter or individual plates and scatter with the remaining parsley. Serve with plenty of fresh French bread.

To make aïoli, work 4 crushed garlic cloves and ½ teaspoon salt into a smooth paste. Scrape into a bowl and add 1 medium egg yolk and 2 teaspoons lemon juice. Whisk together with an electric whisk, then very gradually whisk in the 175ml olive oil to make a thick mayonnaise-like mixture.

Serves 6

1.5kg (3lb 5oz) small clams, small mussels or cockles, or a mixture

150ml (¼ pint) dry white wine

500g (1lb) cooked shell-on North Atlantic prawns, heads removed but not the rest of the shell

aïoli (see below)

3 tbsp freshly chopped flat-leaf parsley

plenty of fresh French bread

Warm Oysters with Champagne Sabayon

As someone who formerly eschewed cooked oysters in favour of oysters au naturel with lemon and nothing else, I feel a bit of a hypocrite including a recipe for them very lightly cooked with a fluffy sabayon. But, they are delicious – you bite through the crisp batter into the salty sea taste of an oyster.

Serves 2

8 oysters

for the champagne sabayon

200ml (7fl oz) champagne

pinch of caster sugar

3 egg yolks

75g (3oz) clarified butter, warmed

a little cayenne pepper

Step one Preheat the grill to high. Open the oysters and pour away the juices from each one (see page 40 for how to open). Put them, still in their half shells, onto a large grilling tray, cover with clingfilm and set to one side.

Step two Put the champagne and sugar into a small pan, bring to the boil and boil rapidly until reduced to 4 tablespoons. Pour into a large heatproof bowl and leave to cool. Add the egg yolks, place the bowl over a pan of barely simmering water and whisk vigorously until the mixture has increased enormously in volume, is thick, light and frothy, and leaves behind a trail when drizzled over the surface.

Step three Remove the bowl from the heat and very slowly whisk in the warm clarified butter. Season to taste with a little salt.

Step four Spoon 1 tablespoon of the champagne sabayon over each oyster and very lightly sprinkle each one with a small pinch of cayenne pepper. Place under the grill for about 30 seconds until lightly browned, and then divide the oysters between two plates and serve immediately.

To make clarified butter, place the butter in a small pan and leave it over a very low heat until it has melted. Skim off any scum from the surface and pour off the clear (clarified) butter into a bowl, leaving behind the milky white solids that will settle on the bottom of the pan.

John Dory Chowder with Mussels and Cider

I love white chowders, the creamy fish soups from New England. Here, my Cornish version contains some local cider, mussels (perfect if you can gather some from a beach somewhere as they are always pleasingly salty) and John Dory, which is firm, well-flavoured and a very special fish from the West Country.

Step one Put the cleaned mussels and cider into a medium-sized pan over a high heat. Cover and cook for 2–3 minutes or until they have just opened, shaking the pan occasionally. Tip them into a colander set over a bowl to collect the juices, and remove any that have not opened. Leave to cool slightly and then remove the meats from the shells, cover and set aside. Discard the shells.

Step two Melt the butter in another pan, add the bacon and fry until lightly golden. Add the onion and cook gently for 5 minutes or until the onion has softened.

Step three Stir in the flour and cook for 1 minute. Gradually stir in the milk and then add all but the last tablespoon or two of the mussel cooking liquor (the last drops might be a bit gritty). Add the potatoes and bay leaf and 1 level teaspoon of salt, and leave to simmer gently for 10 minutes or until the potatoes are just tender.

Step four Remove the bay leaf, add the pieces of John Dory and simmer for 2–3 minutes or until the fish is just cooked. Stir in the double cream and season to taste with cayenne pepper, salt and white pepper.

Step five Remove from the heat and stir in the mussels, to warm them through briefly, and most of the chopped parsley. Serve in warmed bowls, sprinkled with the remaining parsley.

Serves 4

500g (1lb) mussels, cleaned

150ml (¼ pint) Cornish cider

25g (1oz) butter

100g (4oz) piece of rindless smoked streaky bacon, cut into small cubes

1 small onion, finely chopped

20g (¾oz) plain flour

1 litre (1¾ pints) full-cream milk

2 potatoes (about 225g /8oz in total), peeled and cubed

1 bay leaf

225g (8oz) John Dory fillet, cut into short, chunky strips

120ml (4fl oz) double cream

pinch of cayenne pepper

salt and freshly ground white pepper

2 tbsp freshly chopped parsley

Marinated Tuna with Passion fruit, Lime and Coriander

This is a very good dish to start quite an elaborate meal for a number of people, because you can slice the tuna and have it arranged on plates in the fridge and just add the dressing at the last minute. It's a good idea to leave the dressing on the fish for 10 minutes, just to start the acid in the lime and passion-fruit 'cooking' the fish, but don't leave it for longer because it then becomes less fresh-tasting.

Serves 4

3cm (1⅛ inch) thick piece of tuna loin fillet, weighing about 400g (14oz)

2 small, ripe and wrinkly passion fruit, each weighing about 35g (1¼ oz)

1 tbsp lime juice

3 tbsp sunflower oil

1 medium-hot green chilli, deseeded and finely chopped

1 tsp caster sugar

1½ tbsp finely chopped coriander

Step one Put the piece of tuna loin fillet onto a board and slice it across, in very thin slices. Lay the slices, side by side but butted close up together, over the base of four large plates. Cover each one with clingfilm and chill for at least 1 hour, or until you are ready to serve.

Step two Shortly before serving, make the marinating dressing. Cut the passion fruit in half and scoop the pulp into a sieve set over a bowl. Rub the pulp through the sieve to extract the juice, and discard the seeds. You should be left with about one tablespoon of juice. Stir in the lime juice, sunflower oil, green chilli, sugar, coriander, ½ teaspoon salt and some freshly ground pepper.

Step three To serve, uncover the plates, spoon over the dressing and spread it over the surface of the fish with the back of the spoon. Leave for 10 minutes before serving.

Tuna Carpaccio with a Mustard Dressing, Capers, Tomato and Mint

The Sicilians make carpaccio with both tuna and swordfish. They are particularly fond of lightly smoked swordfish presented like this, although I tend to think salmon is a much better fish for smoking. But they do have excellent tuna.

Step one Trim the piece of tuna to remove any blood-red flesh and sinews and to give it a nice shape. Wrap it tightly in some clingfilm and place it in the freezer for about 3 hours until it is firm but not completely frozen.

Step two Remove the tuna from the freezer, unwrap and place on a chopping board. Cut the tuna across into very thin slices using a very sharp, long-bladed knife.

Step three Arrange about four slices of the tuna in a single layer over the base of four cold plates, pressing the slices out slightly so that they butt up together.

Step four For the mustard dressing, whisk the mustard and vinegar together in a small bowl then whisk in the oil 1 teaspoon at a time so that it forms a thick, well-emulsified dressing. Whisk in a few drops of warm water to loosen it slightly and season to taste with some salt and pepper.

Step five Using a teaspoon, drizzle the mustard dressing over the tuna in a zigzag fashion. Then scatter some of the diced tomato, capers, shredded mint and parsley over each plate. Sprinkle with some sea salt flakes and black pepper and serve immediately.

Serves 4

225g (8oz) piece of tuna loin fillet, taken from towards the tail end to measure about 10cm (4in) across

1 ripe vine tomato, skinned, deseeded and cut into small dice

1 tsp small capers, drained and rinsed

4 mint leaves, very finely shredded

4 flat-leaf parsley leaves, finely shredded

for the mustard dressing

1 tsp Dijon mustard

1 tsp white wine vinegar

2 tbsp extra-virgin olive oil

Ceviche of Monkfish with Avocado

Lara Skinner, who is an effervescent member of our staff at St Petroc's, comes from Peru and says we can never get ceviche totally right because we don't have the same limes. I think this is a pretty good attempt actually.

Serves 6

500g (1lb) monkfish fillets

juice of 3 limes

1 medium-hot red chilli, halved and deseeded

1 small red onion

6 vine-ripened tomatoes, skinned (see page 39)

3 tbsp extra-virgin olive oil

2 tbsp freshly chopped coriander

1 large ripe but firm avocado

Step one Cut the monkfish fillets across into thin slices and put them into a shallow dish. Pour over the lime juice, making sure that all the slices of fish are completely coated in juice. Cover with clingfilm and chill for 40 minutes, during which time the fish will turn white and opaque.

Step two Meanwhile, slice across each chilli half so that you get very thin, slightly curled slices. Cut the onion into quarters and then cut each wedge lengthways into thin, arc-shaped slices. Cut each tomato into quarters and remove the seeds. Cut each piece of flesh lengthways into thin, arc-shaped slices.

Step three Just before you are ready to serve, lift the monkfish out of the lime juice with a slotted spoon and put into a large bowl with the chilli, onion, tomato, olive oil, most of the coriander and a little salt to taste. Toss together lightly.

Step four Halve the avocado, remove the stone and peel. Slice each half lengthways into thin slices. Arrange 3–4 slices of the avocado on one side of each plate. Pile the ceviche onto the other side and sprinkle with the rest of the coriander. Serve immediately.

Gravlax (Dill-cured Salmon)

I like a thick, green crust of dill and peppercorns, as it looks so appetising when the salmon is sliced and served with some of the mustard and horseradish sauce alongside. You might like to serve the gravlax with some boiled new potatoes to make a more substantial course.

Step one Put one of the salmon fillets, skin side down, onto a large sheet of clingfilm. Mix the dill with the salt, sugar and crushed peppercorns and spread it over the cut face of the salmon. Place the other fillet on top, skin side up.

Step two Tightly wrap the fish in two or three layers of clingfilm and lift it onto a large, shallow tray. Rest a slightly smaller tray or chopping board on top of the fish and weigh it down. Chill for 2 days, turning the fish every 12 hours so the briny mixture that will develop inside the parcel bastes the fish.

Step three To make the horseradish and mustard sauce, stir together all the ingredients except the cream. Whip the cream into soft peaks, stir in the horseradish mixture, cover and chill.

Step four To serve, remove the fish from the briny mixture and slice it very thinly, as you would smoked salmon. Arrange a few slices of the gravlax on each plate and serve with some of the sauce.

Serves 6

2 x 750g (1lb 10oz) unskinned salmon fillets

large bunch of dill, roughly chopped

100g (4oz) coarse sea salt

75g (3oz) caster sugar

2 tbsp crushed white peppercorns

for the horseradish and mustard sauce

2 tsp finely grated horseradish (fresh or from a jar)

2 tsp finely grated onion

1 tsp Dijon mustard

1 tsp caster sugar

2 tbsp white wine vinegar

good pinch of salt

175ml (6fl oz) double cream

Have you made this recipe? Tell us what you think at
www.mykitchentable.co.uk/blog

KITCHEN
TABLE

The Padstow Deli Crab Sandwich with Parsley, Chilli, Lemon and Rocket

If crab came out of its shell in lovely firm pieces like lobster, I wouldn't be surprised if it fetched more money, because I often think it's got a better flavour than lobster. Fortunately, crab is not enormously expensive and it's really good in sandwiches. This is a great favourite at our deli.

Makes 6

12 thin slices of wholemeal bread

75g (3oz) butter, softened

5 tbsp mayonnaise (see page 39)

1 tsp fresh lemon juice

½–1 red chilli, depending on heat, deseeded and finely chopped

500g (1lb) fresh hand-picked white crabmeat

2 tbsp freshly chopped flat-leaf parsley

50g (2oz) rocket

Step one Butter the slices of bread and put them to one side.

Step two Put the mayonnaise into a small bowl and stir in the lemon juice and chilli. Put the crabmeat and parsley into another bowl and lightly stir through the mayonnaise mixture. Season to taste with a little salt.

Step three Put six slices of the bread, buttered sides up, on a board and spoon over the crab mixture. Cover with a generous layer of the rocket leaves and then top with the remaining slices of bread. Cut each sandwich diagonally into halves or quarters and serve immediately.

Hugo's Breakfast Fishcakes

I was once asked to rename this recipe but couldn't possibly because it's Hugo's. He runs a brilliant guesthouse just outside Padstow called Woodlands, where he cooks special breakfasts.

Step one Cook the prepared potatoes in boiling, salted water for 20 minutes or until tender. Drain well, tip back into the pan and mash until smooth. Set aside.

Step two Meanwhile, put the fish, milk, lemon zest, bay leaf and some black pepper into a pan. Cover, bring to the boil and simmer for 4 minutes or until the fish has just cooked through. Discard the bay leaf and lemon zest, lift the fish onto a plate and reserve the poaching milk. Remove and discard any skin and bones from the fish and leave the fillet to cool slightly.

Step three Melt 15g (½oz) of the butter in a medium-sized pan, add 1 teaspoon of the olive oil and the onion, and cook gently for 6–7 minutes, until soft and translucent but not brown. Add the mashed potatoes and allow them to warm through; then add the fish, parsley, lemon juice and 2 tablespoons of the poaching milk and mix together well. The mixture should be neither dry nor so wet that it is difficult to handle. Leave to cool.

Step four Meanwhile, season the flour with a little salt and pepper and sprinkle it onto the work surface. Put the egg into a shallow dish and the breadcrumbs into another. Using slightly wet hands, form the mixture in the flour into eight fishcakes about 1cm (½in) thick. Dip them into the beaten egg and then the breadcrumbs, put onto a baking tray and chill them for 1 hour(or better still overnight) in the fridge.

Step five Heat the remaining butter and the final teaspoon of oil in a non-stick frying pan until the butter has melted, add the fishcakes and then fry them gently for about 5 minutes on each side until golden. Serve with some soured cream and chives on the side.

Serves 4

400g (14oz) floury main-crop potatoes, such as Desirée, peeled and cut into large chunks

300g (11oz) fillet of white fish, such as pollack, gurnard, cod or haddock, cut into small chunks

225ml (8fl oz) full-fat milk

1 pared strip of lemon zest

1 bay leaf

40g (1½oz) butter

2 tsp olive oil

1 small onion, finely chopped

a handful of freshly chopped curly-leaf parsley

1 tsp fresh lemon juice

25g (1oz) plain flour

1 large egg, beaten

100g (4oz) fresh white breadcrumbs

soured cream and chives, to serve

Devilled Mackerel with Mint and Tomato Salad

I wrote this with the aim of using just the ingredients you would find in the average kitchen cupboard. It's one of my meals-in-minutes dishes and it's very popular.

Serves 4

4 x 350g (12oz) mackerel, cleaned and trimmed

40g (1½ oz) butter

1 tsp caster sugar

1 tsp English mustard powder

1 tsp cayenne pepper

1 tsp paprika

1 tsp ground coriander

2 tbsp red wine vinegar

1 tsp freshly ground pepper

2 tsp salt

for the mint and tomato salad

225g (8oz) small vine-ripened tomatoes, sliced

1 small onion, halved and very thinly sliced

1 tbsp freshly chopped mint

1 tbsp fresh lemon juice

Step one Preheat the grill to high. Slash the skin of the mackerel at 1cm (½in) intervals on both sides from the head all the way down to the tail, taking care not to cut too deeply into the flesh.

Step two Melt the butter in a small roasting tin. Remove from the heat, stir in the sugar, mustard, spices, vinegar, pepper and salt and mix together well. Add the mackerel to the spiced butter and turn them over once or twice until well coated in the mixture, spreading some into the cavity of each fish as well. Transfer them to a lightly oiled baking sheet or the rack of the grill pan and grill for 4 minutes on each side, until cooked through.

Step three Meanwhile, for the salad, layer the sliced tomatoes, onion and mint on four serving plates, and sprinkle the layers with the lemon juice and some seasoning. Put the cooked mackerel alongside and serve, with some fried sliced potatoes if you wish.

Goujons of Lemon Sole with Parmesan Breadcrumbs

I can't think of a better fish for goujons than lemon sole – its flavour seems to complement speedy deep-frying in a breadcrumb coating perfectly – but all of the cheaper flat fish, such as flounder, plaice and dab, are almost improved by deep-frying.

Step one Cut the fish fillets diagonally into strips about 2½cm (1in) across. Mix the breadcrumbs with the grated Parmesan cheese and cayenne pepper and then set aside. Heat some oil for deep-frying to 190°C/375°F or until a cube of day-old bread will brown in about a minute. Line a baking sheet with plenty of kitchen paper.

Step two Coat the goujons a few at a time in the flour, then in beaten egg and finally in the breadcrumb mixture, making sure that they all take on an even coating and remain separate.

Step three Drop a small handful of goujons into the oil and deep-fry for about 1 minute until crisp and golden. Lift out with a slotted spoon onto the paper-lined baking sheet to drain and repeat with the remaining fish, making sure the oil has come back to temperature first.

Step four Pile the goujons onto four warmed plates and garnish with the lemon wedges. If you like, serve with a mixed whole leaf or herb salad, simply dressed with a little extra-virgin olive oil and some seasoning.

Serves 4

450g (1lb) skinned lemon sole fillets

100g (4oz) fresh white breadcrumbs

25g (1oz) Parmesan cheese, finely grated

½ tsp cayenne pepper

sunflower oil, for deep-frying

50g (2oz) plain flour

3 eggs, beaten

lemon wedges, to serve

Eggs Benedict with Smoked Haddock

This is my favourite breakfast dish – wonderfully luxurious. Use only the very best, freshest smoked haddock, and preferably undyed.

Serves 4

300ml (½ pint) milk

3 bay leaves

2 slices onion

6 black peppercorns

4 x 100g (4oz) pieces of thick, undyed smoked haddock fillet

1 tbsp white wine vinegar

4 eggs

2 English muffins

good-quality hollandaise sauce, to serve

to garnish

coarsely crushed black peppercorns

a few snipped fresh chives

Step one If making the hollandaise sauce, do this now (see below). Keep it warm, off the heat, over a pan of warm water Bring the milk and 300ml (½ pint) of water to the boil in a shallow pan. Add the bay leaves, onion, peppercorns and smoked haddock pieces, bring back to a simmer and poach for 4 minutes. Lift the haddock out onto a plate, peel off the skin and keep warm.

Step two Bring about 5cm (2in) of water to the boil in a medium-sized pan, add the vinegar and reduce it to a gentle simmer. Break the eggs into the pan one at a time and poach for 3 minutes. Meanwhile, slice the muffins in half and toast them until lightly browned. Lift the poached eggs out with a slotted spoon and drain briefly on kitchen paper.

Step three To serve, place the muffin halves onto four warmed plates and top with the haddock and poached eggs. Spoon over the hollandaise sauce and garnish with a sprinkling of crushed black pepper and chopped chives.

To make hollandaise sauce, put 2 tablespoons of water and 2 egg yolks into a stainless steel or glass bowl set over a pan of simmering water, making sure the base of the bowl is not touching the water. Whisk until voluminous and creamy. Remove the bowl from the pan and gradually whisk in 225g (8oz) warmed clarified butter until thick (see page 44). Whisk in the juice of ½ lemon, cayenne pepper and salt. This will make enough to serve 4.

For a video masterclass on poaching an egg, go to
www.mykitchentable.co.uk/videos/poachingegg

KITCHEN
TABLE

Jack's Mud Crab Omelette

Jack was a customer at Two Small Rooms, a delightful restaurant in Brisbane, Australia, that I used to visit too. He visited the restaurant every Saturday night and ordered this omelette every time, followed by a steak.

Step one To make the sauce, put the lime juice and garlic into a liquidiser and whizz until smooth. Add all the remaining sauce ingredients and blend well. Add enough water to make a smooth, sauce-like consistency, then pass through a fine sieve.

Step two For the vegetable stir-fry, heat the oil in a frying pan or wok, add all the vegetables and stir-fry for 1–2 minutes until just cooked but still crunchy. Add the pickled ginger and toss for a few seconds to heat through.

Step three Drizzle some of the nam prik sauce over each serving plate in a zigzag pattern and then put the stir-fried vegetables in the centre of each plate.

Step four For the omelettes, heat a 20–23cm (8–9in) omelette pan over a medium heat, add 1 tablespoon of the oil and, when it is hot, a quarter of the beaten eggs. Move the mixture over the base of the pan with the back of a fork until it begins to set, then stop stirring and cook until it is just a little moist on top – about 2 minutes in total. Put a quarter of the crab meat down the centre of the omelette and season to taste with salt and pepper. Fold the sides of the omelette over the crab meat and place on the stir-fried vegetables. Serve immediately and cook the remaining omelettes in the same way.

Serves 4

for the nam prik sauce

juice of 1 lime

1 large garlic clove

1 tbsp Thai sweet chilli and dried shrimp sauce

½ tsp Indonesian red chilli paste

25ml (1fl oz) ketjap manis (sweet soy sauce)

100g (4oz) light muscovado sugar

2 tbsp chopped coriander

1 tsp chopped mint

for the vegetable stir-fry

1 tbsp sunflower oil

40g (1½ oz) beansprouts

40g (1½ oz) mangetout, thinly shredded

½ red pepper, cut into strips

½ medium carrot, cut into strips

½ red onion, sliced

4 fresh shiitake mushrooms, thinly sliced

4 oyster mushrooms, torn into fine strips

15g (½ oz) Japanese pickled ginger, shredded

for the omelettes

4 tbsp sunflower oil

12 large eggs, beaten

225g (8oz) fresh white crabmeat

Japanese Fishcakes with Ginger and Spring Onions

This refreshing recipe works equally well with other types of oily fish, such as herring, mackerel and salmon.

Serves 4

3 rainbow trout, filleted (about 600g/1lb 2oz fillets in total)

4cm (1½in) piece of fresh root ginger, very finely chopped

3 fat spring onions, finely chopped

4 chestnut mushrooms, finely chopped

a little oil, for frying

for the salad

100g (4oz) rocket

2 tsp dark soy sauce

1 tsp roasted sesame oil

1 tsp cold water

pinch of caster sugar

Step one Skin and then pin-bone the trout fillets, and then cut them lengthways into long, thin strips. Now bunch these strips together and cut them across into very small pieces – you should not work the fish into a very fine paste, but neither should it be too coarse, or it won't hold together.

Step two Put the fish into a mixing bowl with the ginger, spring onions, mushrooms and some salt and pepper. Mix together well and then divide the mixture into eight and, with slightly wet hands, shape into patties about 7½cm (3in) in diameter.

Step three Heat a lightly oiled, non-stick frying pan over a medium heat. Add the fishcakes and fry for about 1½ minutes on each side, until golden brown and cooked through. Put onto warmed plates and pile some of the rocket alongside. Whisk together the remaining salad ingredients to make a dressing, and drizzle some over the rocket and a little around the outside edge of the plates.

Crab with Rocket, Basil and Lemon Olive Oil

This is based on my memory of a dish from Assaggi, a modern Italian restaurant above a pub in London's Notting Hill. It is light, lively and perfectly composed for bringing the best out of fresh white crabmeat.

Step one Put the crabmeat in a bowl and gently stir in the lemon juice, olive oil, basil and some seasoning to taste.

Step two Make a small, tall pile of the crab mixture on four plates, placing them slightly off centre. Put a small pile of rocket leaves alongside. Drizzle a little more olive oil over the rocket and around the outside edge of the plates. Sprinkle the oil with a little sea salt and cracked black pepper and serve.

Serves 4

350g (12oz) fresh hand-picked white crabmeat

2 tsp fresh lemon juice

4 tsp extra-virgin olive oil, preferably lemon olive oil (see page 143), plus extra for drizzling

8 basil leaves, finely shredded

a handful of wild rocket leaves

sea salt and cracked black pepper, to garnish

Chargrilled Snapper with an Avocado, Mango, Prawn and Chilli Salsa

This recipe works well cooked under the grill or on the barbecue. You could use red mullet, sea bass, bream or John Dory instead of snapper.

Serves 4

4 x 175g (6oz) pieces of unskinned snapper fillet

extra-virgin olive oil

coriander sprigs, to garnish

for the salsa

2 large medium-hot red Dutch chillies

100g (4oz) peeled cooked tiger prawns, thickly sliced

4 spring onions, thinly sliced

1 small garlic clove, finely chopped

1 ripe but firm avocado, peeled and cut into small dice

½ ripe but firm mango, peeled and cut into small dice

juice of 1 lime

Step one If you are using a barbecue, light it 30–40 minutes before you want to cook the fish.

Step two To make the salsa, cut the chillies in half lengthways and scrape out the seeds with the tip of a small knife but leave the ribs behind to give the salsa a little more heat. Cut the chillies into thin slices then simply mix all the ingredients together.

Step three If you are not cooking the fish on a barbecue, put a ridged cast-iron griddle over a high heat or preheat the grill to high. Brush the snapper fillets on both sides with olive oil and season well with salt and pepper. Cut each fillet into three, slightly on the diagonal.

Step four Cook the pieces of snapper either skin-side down on the griddle or barbecue, or skin-side up under the grill, for 3–4 minutes.

Step five To serve, spoon the salsa onto four plates and arrange the grilled strips of fish on top. Drizzle a little oil around the edge of the plates and garnish with coriander sprigs.

Mackerel Recheado with Katchumber Salad

I often think this is the best way to serve mackerel. There is something about the way the oily fish and the flavours of the garlic, ginger, Kashmiri chilli, onion, tamarind and spices blend together that is endlessly pleasing.

Step one If you are cooking the mackerel on the barbecue, light it 40 minutes before you are ready to cook. Make the paste for the fish (see page 76)

Step two Prepare the mackerel. Cut the heads off the mackerel. Start to cut away the top fillet until you can get the whole blade of the knife underneath. Rest a hand on top of the fish and cut the fillet away from the bones until you are about 2½cm (1in) away from the tail.

Step three Turn the fish over and repeat on the other side. Pull back the top fillet and snip out the backbone, close to the tail, with scissors. The fillets will still be attached at the tail. Spread the cut face of one fillet with a tablespoon of the masala paste. Push the fish back into shape and tie in two places with string. If you are grilling the mackerel, preheat the grill to high.

Step four To make the katchumber salad, layer all the ingredients in a shallow dish. Barbecue or grill the mackerel for 3–4 minutes on each side until crisp and lightly golden. Lift them onto four warmed plates. Serve with some of the katchumber salad, and some pilau rice.

Serves 4

4 x 225g (8oz) mackerel

Goan masala paste (see page 76)

for the katchumber salad

450g (1lb) vine-ripened tomatoes, thinly sliced

1 red onion, quartered and thinly sliced

2 tbsp roughly chopped coriander leaves

¼ tsp ground cumin

pinch of cayenne pepper

1 tbsp white wine vinegar

¼ tsp salt

Sardine and Potato Curry Puffs

These would also work well with mackerel, pilchards, sprats, herrings and any other oily fish with lots of flavour.

Makes 12

100g (4oz) potatoes, cut into 1cm (½ in) cubes

1 tbsp sunflower oil, plus extra for deep-frying

2 garlic cloves, crushed

1cm (½ in) piece of fresh root ginger, finely grated

½ onion, thinly sliced

1 tbsp Goan masala paste (see below)

225g (8oz) sardines, cleaned, filleted and cut across into strips 2½ cm (1in) wide

1 medium-hot red chilli, deseeded and finely chopped

1 tbsp fresh lemon juice

¼ tsp salt

2–3 spring onions, sliced

2 tbsp freshly chopped coriander

450g (1lb) puff pastry

to garnish

lemon wedges

coriander sprigs

Step one Boil the potato in salted water until just tender, then drain. Heat the oil in a large frying pan and fry the garlic, ginger and onion for 1 minute. Add the Goan masala paste and fry for 1 minute, then add the pieces of sardine and fry for a further minute. Finally, put in the potato, chilli, lemon juice and salt and cook for 1 minute. Take the pan off the heat, stir in the spring onions and coriander and leave to cool.

Step two Roll out the pastry on a lightly floured surface and cut out twelve 10cm (4in) circles. Spoon a heaped teaspoon of the filling mixture onto each circle. Brush half of the pastry edge with a little water, then fold it over the filling and press together well to seal the edge. Mark along the edge with a fork to make an even tighter seal.

Step three Heat some oil for deep-frying to 190°C/375°F or until a cube of day-old bread rises to the surface and browns in about a minute. Deep-fry the puffs three or four at a time for 7–8 minutes, turning them over every now and then until they are golden brown. Drain on kitchen paper.

Step four Keep warm in a low oven while you cook the rest. Pile them onto a plate and serve warm, garnished with some lemon wedges and coriander.

To make Goan masala curry paste, grind together 1 teaspoon each of cumin seeds, coriander seeds and black peppercorns, ½ teaspoon each of fennel seeds, cloves and turmeric powder into a fine powder using a spice grinder. Put the powder into a food processor and add 50g (2oz) roughly chopped medium-hot red chillies, 1 teaspoon of light muscovado sugar, 3 chopped garlic cloves, 1½ teaspoons of tamarind water (see page 12), 2½ cm (1in) fresh root ginger and 1 tablespoon of red wine vinegar. Blend into a smooth paste.

Fried Gurnard with Sweet and Sour Red Onions

The secret with the accompaniment here is to cook the onions only long enough that they still have a subtle al dente bite, and to use red wine vinegar, and honey instead of sugar for the sweetness.

Step one To make the sweet and sour onions, heat the olive oil in a frying pan. Add the onions, vinegar, honey, ½ teaspoon salt and some pepper and cook gently for 10 minutes, stirring every now and then, until the onions are soft but still with a little bite. Do not let them brown. Keep warm.

Step two Pour the olive oil for shallow frying into a wide shallow pan to a depth of 1cm (½in) and heat it to 180°C/350°F. Season the fish fillets on both sides with salt and pepper and then coat them in the plain flour and knock off the excess. Reduce the heat slightly under the pan, add the fish fillets and cook them for 1 minute on each side until lightly golden and cooked through. Lift onto kitchen paper and drain briefly.

Step three Overlap two fish fillets in the centre of a warmed plate and spoon over some of the sweet and sour onions and capers.

Serves 4

olive oil, for shallow frying

8 x 75g (3oz) gurnard fillets

50g (2oz) plain flour

1 tsp small capers, to garnish

for the sweet and sour onions

50ml (2fl oz) extra-virgin olive oil

2 medium red onions, halved and thinly sliced

2 tbsp red wine vinegar

2 tbsp clear honey

Sashimi of Salmon, Tuna, Sea Bass and Scallops

The size and shape of the fish fillets are crucial to the finished look of this dish. The salmon and sea bass should both come from reasonably sized fish where the fillets are between 2.5cm (1in) and 4cm (1½in) thick. The tuna is a little more difficult to achieve. You need to buy a piece of loin that is about 10cm (4in) long, cut from the thicker end of the fillet, and then cut it lengthways into about three long, narrow pieces that are each about 5cm (2in) across.

Serves 4

90g (3¼ oz) piece skinned salmon fillet, pin bones removed

90g (3¼ oz) piece sea bass fillet, skinned and pin bones removed

90g (3¼ oz) piece tuna fillet

4 scallops, out of the shell, corals removed

for the dipping sauce

3 tbsp dashi

3 tbsp mirin

3 tbsp light soy sauce

for the garnish

1 x 7.5cm (3in) piece daikon radish (mooli), peeled and finely shredded lengthways on a mandolin

wasabi paste

Japanese pickled ginger

Step one Carefully trim away the brown meat from the skinned side of the salmon fillet. Then, using a very sharp knife, neatly trim up all the fish fillets to remove any thin pieces of fish, then cut each one across into 5mm (¼in) thick slices. Cut each scallop horizontally into three slices.

Step two Mix the ingredients for the dipping sauce together and divide between four small dipping saucers.

Step three To serve, arrange each type of fish, overlapping the slices very slightly, attractively on each plate and put the daikon, a hazelnut-sized amount of wasabi, some pickled ginger and a little saucer of dipping sauce alongside. Serve with chopsticks.

To make 1 litre of dashi, put 1 litre (¾ pint) water and 1 x 10cm (4in) piece dried kombu seaweed into a small saucepan and heat to just below boiling point. Remove from the heat and leave for 5 minutes, then lift out and discard the kombu. Bring the liquid back to a simmer, add 15g (⅛ oz) bonito flakes and bring up to the boil. Remove the pan from the heat and leave the flakes to settle for 1 minute. Then pour through a very fine muslin-lined sieve into a bowl. The dashi is now ready to use.

Warm Mussel and Potato Salad with Pistou

The recipe for the pistou (French Provençal pesto) makes a bit more than required, but it's difficult to make in smaller amounts. Store it in a screw-top jar in the fridge and use within two to three days; it's great stirred into vegetable soups or pasta.

Step one Peel the potatoes and put them into a pan of cold salted water (1 teaspoon per 600ml/1 pint). Bring to the boil and cook for 12–15 minutes until tender. Drain, return to the pan, cover and keep warm.

Step two To make the pistou, blend the basil, garlic, tomato and Parmesan cheese into a food processor. With the machine still running, gradually add the oil to make a mayonnaise-like mixture. Season to taste with ¼ teaspoon of salt and some black pepper.

Step three Put the mussels and 2 tablespoons of water into a medium-sized pan, cover and place over a high heat. Cook for 2–3 minutes, shaking the pan once or twice, until the mussels have just opened. Tip into a colander set over a bowl to collect the juices, discarding any that have not opened, and when they are cool enough to handle, remove all but a few of them from the shells. Cover and keep warm. Return the mussel cooking liquor to the pan and rapidly boil until reduced and well flavoured.

Step four Put 4 tablespoons of the pistou into a small bowl and stir in 2 teaspoons of the reduced mussel cooking liquor to loosen it slightly.

Step five Mix the frisée with the rocket and divide between four plates. Slice the potatoes and arrange them in among the leaves, along with the mussels. Drizzle over the loosened pistou, squeeze over a little lemon juice and serve immediately, while the potatoes are still warm.

Serves 4

350g (12oz) small waxy potatoes

750g (1lb 10oz) medium-sized mussels, cleaned

50g (2oz) prepared frisée (curly endive)

50g (2oz) wild rocket

¼ lemon, for squeezing

for the pistou

50g (2oz) fresh basil leaves

3 fat garlic cloves, peeled

75g (3oz) vine-ripened tomato, skinned, deseeded and chopped

75g (3oz) Parmesan cheese, finely grated

150ml (¼ pint) olive oil

Seared Scallops with Lentils and a Tomato and Herbes de Provence Dressing

Everybody loves seared scallops. The problem is that in many restaurants they are partnered with things that leave you wondering why: large lumps of black pudding, potato choux balls, ponzu sauce, you name it. Here I've just used a well-reduced tomato dressing with good olive oil, and added a pile of lentils and a squeeze of lemon.

Serves 4

100g (4oz) Puy lentils

2½ tbsp olive oil

12–16 large prepared scallops

for the dressing

7 tbsp extra-virgin olive oil

4 small garlic cloves, finely chopped

4 medium-sized vine tomatoes, skinned, deseeded and chopped

½ tsp chopped mixed rosemary and thyme or large pinch of dried herbes de Provence

2 tbsp red wine vinegar

1 tsp caster sugar

1 tbsp fresh lemon juice

1 tsp freshly chopped basil and parsley

Step one To make the dressing, put 2 tablespoons of the extra-virgin olive oil and the garlic into a small pan, and place over a medium-high heat. As soon as the garlic begins to sizzle, add the tomatoes and chopped rosemary and thyme, or herbes de Provence, and simmer for 10–12 minutes until well reduced and thick. Put the vinegar and sugar into another small pan and boil rapidly until reduced to 2 teaspoons. Stir into the tomato sauce, season to taste with some salt and pepper and set to one side.

Step two Bring a pan of well-salted water to the boil (1 teaspoon per 600ml/1 pint). Add the lentils and cook for 15–20 minutes or until tender. Drain well, return to the pan with ½ tablespoon of the olive oil and some salt and pepper, cover and keep warm.

Step three Slice each scallop horizontally into two discs, leaving the roe attached to one slice. Place in a shallow dish with the remaining 2 tablespoons of olive oil and some salt and pepper.

Step four To finish the tomato dressing, add the remaining 5 tablespoons of extra-virgin olive oil, the lemon juice and some salt to taste and leave to warm through gently over a very low heat. Heat a dry, non-stick frying pan until smoking hot. Reduce the heat slightly, add 1 teaspoon of oil and half the scallop slices and sear them for 1 minute on each side until golden brown. Lift onto a plate and repeat with the rest.

Step five Divide the lentils between four warmed plates and arrange the scallop slices alongside. Stir the chopped basil and parsley into the warm tomato dressing, spoon some over and around the scallops and serve immediately.

Pissaladière (Niçoise Onion Tart)

The combination of sweet onions and salty anchovies on crisp dough, hot from the baker's oven, is a truer reflection of the people and the lifestyle in southern France than any frothy combination of bright colours and flavours. For me, it sums up all that's best about street food.

Step one To make the dough base, sift the flour, yeast and 1 teaspoon salt into a bowl and make a well in the centre. Add the warm water and olive oil and mix together into a soft dough. Tip out onto a lightly floured surface and knead for 5 minutes or until smooth and elastic. Return to the bowl, cover with clingfilm and leave in a warm place for approximately 1 hour, or until doubled in size.

Step two Meanwhile, prepare the topping. Heat the oil in a large pan over a low heat. Add the onions, bouquet garni and some seasoning, cover and cook gently for 45 minutes, stirring occasionally. Uncover, increase the heat a little and continue to cook for 20 minutes or until all the moisture from the onions has evaporated and they are thick and pale brown. Discard the bouquet garni, adjust the seasoning if necessary and set aside.

Step three Preheat the oven to 240°C/475°F/gas 9, or as high as it will go. Turn out the dough onto a lightly floured work surface, knock out the air and knead briefly once more. Then roll it out into a rectangle and lift onto an oiled 30 x 37.5cm (12 x 14½in) baking sheet. Reshape with your fingers, then carefully spread with a thin layer of the anchovy paste. Spread the onion mixture evenly over the top, leaving a 2.5cm (1in) border free all around the edge, then criss-cross the top with the halved anchovy fillets and dot with the black olives. Season lightly with salt and pepper and leave somewhere warm to rise slightly for 10–15 minutes.

Step four Bake for 15–20 minutes, until the crust has browned and the edges of the onions are starting to caramelise. Serve warm or at room temperature, cut into rectangles.

Serves 6–8
275g (10oz) strong plain white flour
2 tsp easy-blend yeast
1 tsp salt
250ml (9fl oz) hand-hot water
2 tsp extra-virgin olive oil

for the topping
50ml (2fl oz) extra-virgin olive oil
1.5kg (3lb 5oz) onions, halved and thinly sliced
a large bouquet garni of fresh parsley, thyme, bay leaves, rosemary and oregano
2 tsp anchovy paste
6–8 anchovy fillets in oil, drained and halved lengthways
a handful of small, black Niçoise olives

Grilled Sardine Croûtes with Tomato, Garlic, Parsley and Olive Oil

Croûtes, grilled rustic bread rubbed with garlic and sprinkled with olive oil, are the French equivalent of the Italian bruschetta. I've taken some of the flavours of a salad Niçoise – hard-boiled eggs, tomato, anchovy and onion – and made it into an appetizing open sandwich. This amount is perfect as a light lunch.

Serves 4

1 red pepper

4 sardines, scaled and trimmed

extra-virgin olive oil, for brushing and drizzling

pinch of crushed dried chillies

4 large slices of rustic white bread, such as Poilâne

1 garlic clove, peeled

1 romaine lettuce heart, broken into separate leaves

4 medium-sized vine-ripened tomatoes, skinned and sliced

1 small red onion, very thinly sliced

2 hard-boiled eggs, sliced

4 anchovy fillets in olive oil, drained

sea salt flakes and freshly ground pepper

Step one Spear the stalk end of the red pepper on a fork and turn the pepper in the flame of a gas burner. Alternatively roast the pepper in a preheated oven (220°C/425°F/gas 7) for about 20-25 minutes, turning once until the skin is black. Leave the pepper to cool. Break it in half and remove the stalks, skin and seeds, then cut into strips.

Step two Preheat the grill to high. To butterfly the sardines, cut off the heads and then open up the gut cavity, clean the insides, and put the fish belly-side down on a chopping board. Press down firmly along the backbone until the fish is flat, then turn the fish over and pull away the backbone, snipping it off at the tail end with scissors. Remove any small bones with tweezers.

Step three Brush the sardines with olive oil and sprinkle lightly on both sides with the crushed dried chillies, some salt and pepper.

Step four Toast the bread. Rub one side of each piece with the garlic clove and put one piece onto each of four plates. Drizzle lightly with olive oil and top each one with a few lettuce leaves, some tomato slices, a few strips of the roasted red pepper and some slices of red onion. Drizzle with a little more oil and season lightly with salt and black pepper.

Step five Put the sardines, skin-side up, onto an oiled baking sheet and grill for 3 minutes. Place on top of the salad-covered bread on each plate, top with the eggs and anchovies and season with a little more salt. Rest the second pieces of bread alongside and serve immediately.

Grilled Prawns with Ouzo, Tomatoes, Chilli and Feta

I like the idea of a recipe whose origins are not lost in the mists of time, and this has a very 1960s feel about it. The combination of ouzo, a well-flavoured tomato sauce and some feta served with some, preferably, barbecued prawns (although you can do them under the grill too) is irresistible.

Step one Put the olive oil and garlic into a frying pan and place over a medium-high heat. As soon as the garlic begins to sizzle around the edges, add the onion and crushed dried chillies and cook gently until softened but not browned. Add the tomatoes and 2 tablespoons of the ouzo and simmer for 7–10 minutes until thickened slightly. Season well with salt and pepper and keep hot.

Step two You can either barbecue or grill the prawns. If you are using a charcoal barbecue, light it 40 minutes before you want to start cooking. If you are using a gas barbecue or grill, turn it on 10 minutes beforehand.

Step three Peel the prawns, leaving the last tail segment of the shell in place. Put them into a bowl and toss with the remaining ouzo, ½ teaspoon salt and some freshly ground pepper. Set aside for 5 minutes. Thread the prawns onto pairs of parallel thin skewers – this will stop them from spinning round when you come to turn them. Brush them lightly with olive oil and barbecue or grill for 1½ minutes on each side until cooked through.

Step four Stir half the feta cheese into the tomato sauce along with the chopped wild fennel herb and spoon it over the base of one large or four individual warmed serving dishes. Push the prawns off the skewers onto the top of the sauce and sprinkle with the remaining feta. Garnish with the fennel sprigs and serve hot.

Serves 4 as a starter or 8 as part of a mixed mezze

3 tbsp olive oil

4 garlic cloves, crushed

1 small onion, finely chopped

½ tsp crushed dried chillies

600g (1lb 5oz) chopped tomatoes

3 tbsp ouzo or Pernod, plus extra for sprinkling

1 kg (2lb 4oz) large raw, shell-on prawns

a little olive oil, for brushing

175g (6oz) Greek feta cheese, crumbled

a small handful of wild fennel herb, roughly chopped

wild fennel herb sprigs, to garnish

Grilled Squid and Chorizo Salad with Garlic, Rocket, Tomatoes and Chickpeas

Choose a small, thin type of chorizo sausage, rather than those the size of a salami.

Serves 4

100g (4oz) dried chickpeas, soaked overnight

300g (10½oz) prepared medium-sized squid or cuttlefish

8 cherry tomatoes, quartered

1½ tbsp fresh lemon juice

6 tbsp extra-virgin olive oil

1 medium-hot red chilli, deseeded and thinly sliced across

2 garlic cloves, finely chopped

a small handful of freshly chopped flat-leaf parsley

50g (2oz) chorizo picante (hot chorizo sausage), cut into thin slices

15–20g (½–¾oz) rocket

Step one Drain the soaked chickpeas, put them into a pan and cover with fresh cold water. Bring to the boil and simmer until the skins begin to crack and the chickpeas are tender – about 40 minutes – adding 1 teaspoon of salt to the pan 5 minutes before the end of the cooking time. Drain and leave to cool.

Step two Cut the body pouch of each squid open along one side and score the inner side with the tip of a small, sharp knife into a fine diamond pattern. Then cut each pouch lengthways in half, then across into 7.5cm (3in) pieces. Separate the tentacles into bite-size pieces.

Step three Stir the tomatoes into the chickpeas along with the lemon juice, 4 tablespoons of the olive oil, the chilli, garlic, flat-leaf parsley and some salt and pepper to taste.

Step four Heat 1 tablespoon of the remaining olive oil in a large frying pan over a high heat. Add half the squid pieces, scored side facing upwards (this will make them curl attractively), and half the tentacles and sear for 30 seconds, then turn them over and sear for a further 30 seconds until golden brown and caramelised. Season with salt and pepper and remove from the pan.

Step five Repeat with the remaining tablespoon of olive oil and the rest of the squid. Return all the squid to the pan along with the chorizo and toss over a high heat for a further minute. Briefly toss the rocket leaves through the chickpea salad and spoon onto one large or four individual plates. Top with the sautéed squid and chorizo and serve.

Goan Lobster with Cucumber and Lime Salad

Any spiny lobster is ideal for this dish, including the native lobsters of Australia, New Zealand, South Africa, the west coast of America and, for that matter, India.

Step one Preheat the oven to 150°C/300°F/gas 2. Remove the meat from the cooked lobsters: put the lobster belly-side down on to a board and make sure that none of the legs are tucked underneath. Cut it in half, first through the middle of the head between the eyes. Turn either the knife or the lobster around and finish cutting it in half through the tail. Open it up and lift out the tail meat from each half. Remove the intestinal tract from the tail meat. Break off the claws and then break them into pieces at the joints. Crack the shells with a knife. Remove the meat from each of the claw sections in as large pieces as possible. Remove the soft greenish tomalley (liver) and any red roe from the head section of the shell with a teaspoon. Pull out the stomach sac and discard. Place the shells on a baking sheet and then warm them through in the oven.

Step two To make the salad, peel the cucumber and cut it into thick slices. Overlap the cucumber slices on a plate and sprinkle with the juice of one of the limes and some salt. Slice the other lime into wedges and set aside to serve with the lobster.

Step three Heat the oil in a large deep frying pan. Add the onion, garlic, ginger and chillies and fry for about 5 minutes, until soft. Add the Goan masala paste and fry for 2–3 minutes. Fold in the lobster meat and cook gently until it has heated through.

Step four Spoon the mixture back into the lobster shells and serve with the cucumber and lime salad, the lime wedges and maybe some warm naan bread.

Serves 4

2 x 750–900g (1lb10oz–2lb) cooked lobsters

2 tbsp groundnut oil

1 onion, chopped

3 garlic cloves, crushed

2.5cm (1in) fresh root ginger, finely grated

2 green chillies, deseeded and chopped

3 tbsp Goan Masala Paste (see page 76)

for the cucumber and lime salad

1 cucumber

2 limes

North Atlantic Prawn Pilaf

This uses ingredients you can get from any fishmonger or supermarket. It's a nice, gentle dish, ideal for supper with a glass of New Zealand Chardonnay.

Serves 4

800g (1lb 11oz) unpeeled, cooked North Atlantic prawns

50g (2oz) butter

1 small onion, chopped

1 small carrot, roughly chopped

½ tsp tomato purée

900ml (1½ pints) good-quality chicken stock

350g (12oz) Basmati rice

2 shallots, finely chopped

1 garlic clove, very finely chopped

3 cloves

3 green cardamom pods

1 cinnamon stick, broken into four pieces

¼ tsp ground turmeric

3 tbsp freshly chopped coriander

3 plum tomatoes, skinned, deseeded and diced

Step one Peel the prawns but retain the heads and shells. Put the prawns on a plate and set aside.

Step two Heat half the butter in a large pan, add the onion and carrot and fry over a medium heat for 6–7 minutes, until lightly browned. Add the prawn heads and shells and continue to fry for 3–4 minutes. Add the tomato purée and chicken stock, bring to the boil and simmer for 15 minutes. Strain into a measuring jug; if there is more than 600ml (1 pint), return it to the clean pan and boil rapidly until reduced to this amount.

Step three Meanwhile, rinse the rice in a few changes of cold water until the water runs relatively clear. Cover with fresh water and leave to soak for 7 minutes. Drain well.

Step four Melt the remaining butter in a saucepan and add the shallots, garlic, cloves, cardamom pods, cinnamon stick and turmeric and fry gently for 5 minutes. Add the rice and stir well to coat the rice with the spicy butter. Add the stock to the pan, season with salt and bring to the boil, then turn the heat right down to the slightest simmer, put a lid on the pan and leave to simmer for 10 minutes. Don't lift the lid during this time.

Step five Uncover and gently stir in the peeled prawns, coriander, diced tomatoes and some seasoning to taste. Cover again and leave for 5 minutes to warm through. Then spoon into a warmed serving dish and serve.

Crab Linguine with Parsley and Chilli

It's very important that the pasta is cooked perfectly al dente. I've suggested a cooking time of 7–8 minutes, but I always test pasta by biting it. Secondly, when I say 'warm the sauce ingredients through over a gentle heat', I really mean 'gentle' – the temperature should never get much above 60°C/140°F. Lastly, try not to break up the crabmeat if it's fresh and has been hand-picked, because lumps of crab meat folded through the pasta look very appetising.

Step one Cook the pasta in a large pan of boiling, well-salted water (1 teaspoon per 600ml/1 pint) for 7–8 minutes or until it is al dente.

Step two Meanwhile, put all the remaining ingredients into another pan and warm through over a gentle heat.

Step three Drain the pasta, return to the pan along with the sauce and briefly toss together. Season to taste. Divide between four warmed plates and serve immediately.

Serves 4

450g (1 lb) dried linguine or spaghetti

3 vine-ripened tomatoes, skinned, deseeded and chopped

300g (10½ oz) fresh white crabmeat

1 tbsp freshly chopped parsley

1½ tbsp fresh lemon juice

50ml (2fl oz) extra-virgin olive oil

pinch of dried chilli flakes

1 garlic clove, finely chopped

Seafood Lasagne

This is the Italian version of fish pie. Unusually for a fish dish, it tastes just as good when reheated.

Serves 8

550g (1¼ lb) ling, or pollack fillets, skinned

12 sheets (250g/9oz) fresh lasagne

175g (6oz) peeled North Atlantic prawns

225g (8oz) fresh white crabmeat

for the tomato sauce

4 tbsp olive oil

2 onions, finely chopped

2 garlic cloves, finely chopped

2 x 400g tins chopped tomatoes

100ml (3½ fl oz) red wine vinegar

4 tsp caster sugar

a large handful of basil leaves, shredded

for the béchamel sauce

1 large onion, halved

6 cloves

1.2 litres (2 pints) full-fat milk

2 bay leaves

1 tsp black peppercorns

65g (2½ oz) butter

65g (2½ oz) plain flour

4 tbsp double cream

50g (2oz) Parmesan cheese, freshly grated

Step one To make the tomato sauce, heat the oil in a pan, add the onions and garlic and cook gently until softened. Add the tomatoes and simmer gently for 15–20 minutes, stirring now and then, until reduced and thickened. Put the vinegar and sugar into a pan and boil rapidly until reduced to 2 teaspoons. Stir into the tomato sauce and season to taste. Stir in the basil and set aside.

Step two For the béchamel sauce, stud the onion with the cloves and put it into a pan with the milk, bay leaves and peppercorns. Bring to the boil and then set aside for 20 minutes to infuse.

Step three Return the milk to the boil, add the fish fillets and simmer for 8 minutes. Lift the fish onto a plate and strain the milk into a jug. When cool enough to handle, break the fish into large flakes, discarding bones. Bring a large pan of well-salted water (1 teaspoon salt per 600ml/1 pint water) to the boil. Drop in the sheets of lasagne, one at a time, then take the pan off the heat and leave to soak for 5 minutes. Drain and set aside.

Step four Preheat the oven to 200°C/400°F/gas 6. To finish the béchamel sauce, melt the butter in a non-stick pan, add the flour and cook over a medium heat for 1 minute. Reduce the heat and gradually beat in the strained milk, then bring to the boil, stirring. Simmer gently over a low heat for 10 minutes, stirring every now and then. Remove the pan from the heat and stir in the cream, half the Parmesan cheese and some seasoning, to taste.

Step five Arrange a layer of the pasta over the base of a 3½-litre (6 pint) ovenproof dish. Spoon over half the tomato sauce and then scatter over half the flaked white fish, prawns and crabmeat. Spoon over one third of the béchamel sauce and then repeat the layers once more. Finish with a final layer of the pasta and the remaining béchamel sauce. Sprinkle over some Parmesan and bake for 40–50 minutes, until golden and bubbling.

Mussels in Pilau Rice with a Coconut, Cucumber and Tomato Relish

For this recipe, I like to gently sauté the rice in flavoured oil or butter and then cook with liquid for only about 15 minutes, so that the grains remain firm and separate.

Step one Put the mussels and 300ml (10fl oz) water into a large pan, cover and cook over a high heat for 3–4 minutes, shaking the pan every now and then, until the mussels have all just opened. Tip them into a colander set over a bowl to collect the cooking liquor, and discard any that have not opened. Pour all but the last tablespoon or two of the cooking liquor into a measuring jug and make up to 600ml (1 pint) with water, if necessary.

Step two Heat a dry, heavy-based frying pan. Add the cumin seeds and mustard seeds and shake them around for a few seconds until they darken slightly and start to smell aromatic. Remove from the heat. Cut the leek lengthways into long, thin strips, then bunch the strips together and slice them across quite finely. Melt the butter in a 20cm (8in) heavy-based pan. Add the leeks and spices and cook over a medium heat for 2–3 minutes, until the leeks have softened. Add the rice and fry briefly until all the grains are well coated in the butter.

Step three Add the mussel cooking liquor and salt and bring quickly to the boil. Stir once, cover with a tight-fitting lid, reduce the heat to low and cook for 15 minutes. Meanwhile, remove the mussel meats from all but 12 of the shells and season them with a little salt.

Step four Mix the relish ingredients together with a large pinch of salt. Uncover the rice and gently fork in the mussel meats. Garnish with the mussels in their shells and serve with the relish.

Serves 4

1½ kg (3lb 5oz) mussels, cleaned

1 tsp cumin seeds

1 tsp black mustard seeds

1 large leek

50g (2oz) butter

½ tsp ground turmeric

½ tsp dried chilli flakes

350g (12oz) Basmati rice

½ tsp sea salt

for the relish

½ cucumber, peeled, deseeded and diced

2 vine-ripened tomatoes, deseeded and diced

50g (2oz) fresh coconut, peeled and finely grated

1 medium-hot green or red chilli, deseeded and chopped

a small bunch of coriander, roughly chopped

4 tsp lime juice

Grilled Cod with Laksa Noodles

This Asian-themed dish is also excellent made with a thick fillet of snapper or haddock or with a halibut steak.

Serves 4

120ml (4fl oz) sunflower oil

good-quality laksa paste (see below)

450ml (¾ pint) good-quality fish stock

4 x 175–225g (6–8 oz) unskinned cod fillets

50g (2oz) dried medium egg noodles

400ml (14fl oz) coconut milk

100g (4oz) fresh beansprouts

4 spring onions, thinly sliced on the diagonal

a handful of chopped mixed mint, basil and coriander

1 lime, cut into four wedges

for the sambal blachan

2 kaffir lime leaves (optional)

8 medium-hot red chillies, deseeded and sliced

1 tsp salt

1 tsp blachan (dried shrimp paste)

grated zest and juice of 1 lime

Step one To make the sambal blachan, if using lime leaves, remove the spines and shred the leaves finely. Put them in a mini food processor along with the chillies, salt, shrimp paste, lime zest and juice and blend to a paste. Spoon into a small serving bowl. If making your own laksa paste, do this now (see below).

Step two Heat the oil in a large pan, add the laksa paste and fry for 10 minutes, stirring constantly, until it smells very fragrant. Add the stock and simmer for 10 minutes.

Step three Preheat the grill to high. Brush both sides of the cod with sunflower oil and season with salt and pepper. Place on a lightly oiled baking sheet, skin side up, and grill for 8 minutes.

Step four Drop the noodles into a pan of boiling, salted water, cover and remove from the heat. Leave to soak for 4 minutes, then drain. Add the coconut milk to the laksa stock and simmer for 3 minutes. Add the noodles, beansprouts, spring onions and 1 teaspoon of salt.

Step five Spoon the laksa into warmed soup plates and place a piece of cod in the centre of each. Scatter chopped mint, basil and coriander around the edge and then spoon a little of the sambal blachan over the cod. Serve the rest separately, with the lime wedges.

To make laksa paste, cover 25g (1oz) dried shrimps with warm water and leave to soak for 15 minutes. Drain and put into a mini food-processor with 3 roughly chopped medium-hot red chillies, 2 cored and roughly chopped lemongrass stalks, 25g (1oz) unroasted cashew nuts, 2 garlic cloves, 2½cm (1in) peeled and roughly chopped piece of fresh root ginger, 1 teaspoon of turmeric powder, 1 roughly chopped small onion, 1 teaspoon of ground coriander and the juice of 1 lime along with 2 tablespoons of cold water. Blend to a smooth paste.

Seared Scallops with Noodles, Chilli, Garlic and Coriander

What I like about this recipe is the combination of cooked thin egg noodles with seared, caramelised scallops. I flavour this dish simply, with some common Chinese things like garlic, ginger, chilli and soy, and finish it with some coriander and sesame oil. It's the sort of thing they do so well in Australia and New Zealand, being close to Asia.

Step one Bring a pan of lightly salted water to the boil. Add the noodles, turn off the heat and leave the noodles for 4 minutes until cooked. Drain and set aside. Add 1 tablespoon of the oil to a frying pan and heat over a medium-low heat. Add the garlic, chilli and ginger and cook for 3–4 minutes, stirring frequently, until they soften. Remove from the pan and keep to one side.

Step two Heat the frying pan again until hot and add the rest of the oil. Fry the scallop slices on both sides until lightly browned – no more than 20 seconds per side. You need to do this in two batches, making sure the pan is hot between each batch.

Step three Return the garlic, chilli and ginger to the pan, with the noodles and soy sauce, and stir until the noodles are well coated. Add the coriander, sesame oil and scallops, toss gently and serve.

Serves 4

100g (4oz) fine dried egg noodles

2 tbsp sunflower oil

4 garlic cloves, thinly sliced

2 medium-hot red chillies, deseeded and sliced

1cm (½ in) piece of fresh root ginger, cut into slithers

12 large, prepared scallops, halved horizontally

1 tsp dark soy sauce

a handful of coriander leaves, chopped

a few drops of toasted sesame oil

Nasi Goreng with Mackerel

The secret of a good nasi goreng is rice that has been cooked well, so that the grains are separate, and that has been left to cool but not been chilled.

Serves 4

225g (8oz) long grain rice

2 x 175–225g (6–8oz) mackerel, cleaned

2 large eggs

sunflower oil, for frying

6 large shallots, sliced

175g (6oz) peeled, cooked North Atlantic prawns

1 tbsp light soy sauce

5cm (2in) piece of cucumber, quartered lengthways and sliced

4 spring onions, chopped

for the nasi goreng paste

3 tbsp groundnut oil

4 large garlic cloves, roughly chopped

2 large shallots, roughly chopped

15g (½ oz) roasted salted peanuts

6 medium-hot red chillies, chopped

1 tbsp tomato purée

½ tsp blachan (dried shrimp paste)

1 tbsp ketjap manis (sweet soy sauce)

Step one First make the nasi goreng paste: put all the paste ingredients into a food processor and blend. Then cook the rice in boiling, salted water for 15 minutes, until just tender. Drain, rinse well and then spread it out on a tray. Leave to cool.

Step two Preheat the grill to high. Season the mackerel on both sides with salt and pepper. Lay them on a lightly oiled baking sheet or the rack of a grill pan and grill for 4 minutes on each side. Leave them to cool and then flake the flesh into large pieces, discarding the bones.

Step three Next, beat the eggs with salt and pepper and then heat a little oil in a frying pan and make three omelettes. The object is to get them as thin as possible. Cook each one till the egg has lightly set on top, then flip over and cook a few seconds on the other side. Roll the omelettes up and leave them to cool. Then thinly slice the omelettes into strips.

Step four Pour 1cm (½in) of sunflower oil into a frying pan. Add the shallots and fry over a medium heat until crisp and golden brown. Lift them out with a slotted spoon and leave to drain on kitchen paper. Spoon 2 tablespoons of the oil from frying the shallots into a large wok and get it smoking hot. Add 2 tablespoons of the nasi goreng paste and stir-fry for 2 minutes.

Step five Add the cooked rice and stir-fry over a high heat for 2 minutes, until it has heated through. Add the prawns, the strips of omelette, the fried shallots and the flaked mackerel and stir-fry for a further minute. Add the soy sauce, cucumber and most of the spring onions, toss together well and then spoon onto a large, warmed plate. Sprinkle with the remaining spring onions and serve immediately.

Roasted Sea Bass with Pastis and an Arborio Rice Risotto

This is not really a risotto, but a riz pilaf, the ingredients for which are rice, water, salt and a lovely olive oil.

Step one Preheat the oven to 220°C/425°F/gas 7 or as high as your oven will go. Brush each fish inside and out with olive oil and season inside and out with some salt and pepper. Push a small bunch of fennel herb inside the gut cavity of each fish and sprinkle it with a little of the pastis. Spread the remaining fennel herb over a large, oiled baking sheet and place the fish on top. Drizzle the fish with a little more oil and the rest of the pastis and set to one side.

Step two For the risotto, heat the olive oil in a medium-sized pan, add the rice and fry gently for 1 minute. Add the boiling water and the salt, bring back to the boil, cover and cook over a low heat for 20 minutes. Then turn off the heat and leave undisturbed for a further 5 minutes.

Step three After the rice has been cooking for 10 minutes, put the sea bass into the oven and roast them for 15 minutes.

Step four To serve, lift the fish, together with some of the fennel herb, onto four warmed plates. Spoon some of the rice into a lightly oiled rounded mould, such as a non-stick mini pudding basin or ramekin, and press down gently. Turn it out alongside the fish, drizzle a little more extra-virgin olive oil around the edge of the plate and garnish with lemon wedges.

Serves 4

4 x 450g (1lb) sea bass, scaled and gutted

olive oil, for brushing

a large bunch of fennel herb

4 tbsp pastis, such as Pernod or Ricard

lemon wedges, to garnish

for the Arborio rice risotto

3 tbsp olive oil

225g (8oz) Arborio rice

475ml (17fl oz) boiling water

½ tsp salt

Singapore Seafood Noodles

Cooked, peeled North Atlantic prawns, cooked, shelled mussels, white crabmeat, lobster and firm fish such as monkfish or Dover sole fillet are also delicious in this recipe.

Serves 4

25g (1oz) dried shiitake mushrooms

15g (½ oz) dried shrimps (optional)

120ml (4fl oz) hot water

175g (6oz) vermicelli noodles (also known as stir-fry noodles)

2 tbsp sunflower oil

2 fat garlic cloves, finely chopped

2½ cm (1in) piece of fresh root ginger, finely grated

100g (4oz) rindless smoked back bacon, cut into thin strips

1 tbsp good-quality garam masala paste

100g (4oz) squid (pouches), cleaned and thinly sliced

100g (4oz) prepared queen scallops, also known as 'queenies'

175g (6oz) peeled, cooked tiger prawns

3 tbsp dark soy sauce

1 tbsp Chinese rice wine or dry sherry

4 spring onions, thinly sliced

Step one Soak the dried mushrooms and the dried shrimps, if using, in the hot water for 30 minutes, until soft. Drain, reserving the soaking liquid, and thinly slice the mushrooms.

Step two Drop the noodles into a pan of boiling water, cover and take off the heat. Leave to soak for 1 minute, then drain. Toss with a little of the oil, to separate the strands.

Step three Heat the rest of the oil in a large wok. Add the garlic and ginger and stir-fry for a few seconds. Add the bacon, garam masala paste and squid and stir-fry for 2 minutes. Add the mushrooms, dried shrimps and scallops and stir-fry for a further minute. Add the prawns, reserved soaking water, soy sauce and rice wine or sherry, followed by the noodles, and toss together gently over a high heat, using two forks, for about 1 minute, until everything is hot and well mixed. Toss in the spring onions and serve immediately.

Lobster with Ginger, Spring Onions and Soft Egg Noodles

Prepare the whole lobster for deep-frying by removing the stomach sac, intestinal tract, antennae and feeler-like legs, then cutting the tail into three pieces and the claws and head into two pieces each.

Step one Heat some oil for deep-frying to 190°C/375°F. Mix the sugar, dark soy sauce, oyster sauce, sesame oil and Chinese rice wine or sherry together in a small bowl, season with 1 teaspoon salt and a pinch of ground white pepper, and set aside. Bring a large pan of water to the boil for the noodles.

Step two Sprinkle the lobster pieces with 1½ tablespoons of the cornflour and deep-fry, in two or three batches if necessary, for 2 minutes. The larger claw might take longer – about 3 minutes. Lift out and drain on kitchen paper.

Step three Heat the tablespoon of sunflower oil in a wok. Add the garlic, ginger and spring onions and stir-fry for a few seconds. Add the lobster to the wok with the soy sauce mixture and stir-fry for 1 minute. Add the chicken stock, then cover and cook over a medium heat for 2 minutes.

Step four Meanwhile, drop the noodles into the pan of boiling water, cover and remove from the heat. Leave them to soak for 2 minutes, loosening them now and then with some chopsticks or a fork.

Step five Mix the rest of the cornflour with 2 tablespoons of cold water, add to the wok and stir for 1 minute, until the sauce thickens.

Step six Drain the noodles and put them in a large serving dish. Spoon the lobster mixture on top and serve immediately.

Serves 2–3

1 x 750g (1lb 10oz) uncooked lobster prepared for stir-fry

sunflower oil, for deep-frying, plus 1 tbsp

½ tsp caster sugar

1 tbsp dark soy sauce

1 tbsp oyster sauce

1 tsp roasted sesame oil

2 tbsp Chinese rice wine or dry sherry

2 tbsp cornflour

2 garlic cloves, crushed

120g (4½ oz) fresh root ginger, peeled and thinly sliced on a mandolin

90g (3¼ oz) spring onions, cut into 2.5cm (1in) pieces

250ml (9fl oz) good-quality chicken stock

175g (6oz) fresh egg thread noodles

Little Ragoût of Seafood with Fines Herbes, White Wine and Linguine

I picked up the makings of this recipe from a chef called Louis – a Yorkshireman who has lived on the Mediterranean coast of France for seven years. He has an instinctive understanding of the local cuisine.

Serves 4

12–16 cooked langoustines or 100g (4oz) large, freshly cooked, peeled prawns

2 medium-sized squid, cleaned, to yield about 250g (9oz)

450g (1lb) small mussels, cleaned

2 tbsp dry white wine

300ml (½ pint) good-quality chicken stock

150g (5oz) dried linguine

4 tbsp olive oil

25g (1oz) plain flour

small pinch of crushed dried chillies

25g (1oz) butter

2 vine-ripened tomatoes, skinned, deseeded and diced

1 garlic clove, finely chopped

20g (¾oz) parsley, tarragon, chervil and chives, finely chopped

1 tsp fresh lemon juice

Step one Peel the langoustines if using. Cut the squid pouches into thin rings and separate the tentacles into pairs. Bring a pan of well-salted water (1 teaspoon per 600ml/1 pint) to the boil.

Step two Heat a pan over a high heat, add the mussels and the wine, cover and cook for 2–3 minutes or until the mussels have just opened. Tip them into a colander set over a bowl to collect the cooking juices, and, when cool enough to handle, remove the meats from the shells. Cover and set aside.

Step three Pour all but the last tablespoon or two of the mussel cooking liquor (as it might be a bit gritty) into a small pan, add the chicken stock and bring to the boil. Boil rapidly until reduced to 180ml (6fl oz), then turn off the heat and keep warm.

Step four Drop the pasta into the pan of boiling water and cook for 8–9 minutes or until al dente. Drain well, return to the pan with 1 tablespoon of the olive oil, toss, cover and keep warm.

Step five Season the squid, toss with the flour and shake off the excess. Heat a large frying pan over a high heat, add 1 tablespoon of olive oil, half the squid and a few flakes of the dried chillies and fry over a high heat for 1 minute until just cooked. Transfer to a plate and repeat with the rest of the squid.

Step six Pour the stock reduction into the pan in which the squid was cooked, add the butter and the last tablespoon of oil. Add the tomatoes, garlic, herbs, langoustines and lemon juice and toss together briefly until the langoustines have heated through. Add the cooked mussels and squid and toss together for 1 minute. Divide the ragoût between four small soup plates, twist some of the pasta into a pile in the centre of each bowl. Serve immediately.

Provençal Fish Pasta with Fennel Seeds, Anchovies, Tomatoes and Olive Oil

I think it's the combination of the saltiness of the anchovies and the exoticism of the fennel that somehow makes the fillets of fish, all broken up in the pasta, taste sweet and delightful.

Step one Cut the fish fillets across into 2.5cm (1in) strips. Set aside. Halve the tomatoes and squeeze out most of the pips and juice. Roughly chop the remainder.

Step two Bring a large pan of well-salted water (1 teaspoon per 600ml/1 pint) to the boil. Add the pasta and cook for 8–9 minutes or according to the packet instructions, until al dente.

Step three Meanwhile, heat the olive oil in a large frying pan. Add the strips of fish and turn over rapidly in the hot oil, throwing in the garlic, fennel seeds and dried chilli as you do so. Cook for 3 minutes until the fish has turned white but is not completely cooked through. Add the tomatoes and anchovies and stir-fry for a further minute. Season with salt and black pepper and add the parsley. Keep warm.

Step four Drain the pasta well and tip into a large, warmed serving bowl. Pour the sauce on top and toss everything together briefly. Serve immediately, with the green salad.

Serves 4

500g (1lb) skinned fish fillets, such as cod, hake, sea bass or gurnard

4 vine-ripened tomatoes, about 350g (12oz)

400g (14oz) dried long pasta, such as linguine or spaghetti

5 tbsp extra-virgin olive oil

4 garlic cloves, thinly sliced

good pinch of fennel seeds (about ¼ tsp)

good pinch of crushed dried chillies (about ¼ tsp)

4 anchovy fillets in olive oil, drained and chopped

30g (1¼ oz) coarsely chopped flat-leaf parsley

green salad, tossed with a little olive oil, red wine vinegar and salt, to serve

KITCHEN TABLE

Have you made this recipe? Tell us what you think at
www.mykitchentable.co.uk/blog

119

Fish Pie

Try making this with haddock and smoked haddock or, if you live in Australia, substitute flat-head for the unsmoked fish.

Serves 4

1 small onion, thickly sliced

2 cloves

1 bay leaf

600ml (1 pint) milk

300ml (½ pint) double cream

450g (1lb) unskinned cod fillet

225g (8oz) undyed smoked cod or haddock fillet

4 eggs

100g (4oz) butter

45g (1½ oz) plain flour

5 tbsp freshly chopped flat-leaf parsley

freshly grated nutmeg

salt and freshly ground white pepper

1.25kg (2lb 12oz) peeled floury potatoes, such as Maris Piper or King Edward

1 egg yolk

Step one Stud a couple of the onion slices with the cloves. Put the onion slices in a large pan with the bay leaf, 450ml (¾ pint) of the milk, the cream, cod and smoked fish. Bring just to the boil and simmer for 8 minutes. Lift the fish out onto a plate and strain the cooking liquor into a jug. When the fish is cool enough to handle, break it into large flakes, discarding the skin and any bones. Sprinkle it over the base of a shallow 1.75 litre (3 pint) ovenproof dish.

Step two Hard-boil the eggs for 8 minutes, then drain and leave to cool. Peel them, cut into chunky slices and arrange on top of the fish.

Step three Melt half the butter in a pan, add the flour and cook for 1 minute, stirring. Take the pan off the heat and gradually stir in the reserved cooking liquor. Return it to the heat and bring slowly to the boil, stirring all the time. Leave it to simmer gently for 10 minutes to cook out the flour. Remove from the heat once more, stir in the parsley and season with nutmeg, salt and white pepper. Pour the sauce over the fish and leave to cool. Chill in the fridge for 1 hour.

Step four Preheat the oven to 200°C/400°F/gas 6. Boil the potatoes for 15–20 minutes. Drain, mash and add the rest of the butter and the egg yolk. Season with salt and freshly ground white pepper. Beat in enough of the remaining milk to form a soft spreadable mash.

Step five Spoon the potato over the filling and mark the surface with a fork. Bake for 35–40 minutes, until piping hot and golden brown.

Vittorio's Pasta with Clams and Porcini

Vittorio's is a great fish restaurant on the beach at Porto Palo, near Menfi on the south coast of Sicily. I didn't have to find this dish for myself because Vittorio was so keen to tell me everything about it. The combination of the fresh porcini, tomato, chilli, white wine, parsley and some carpet-shell clams (vongole verace) is simply irresistible. If you can't get hold of fresh porcini, use chestnut mushrooms instead together with a few soaked dried porcini.

Step one Bring 4.5 litres (7½ pints) water to the boil in a large pan with 8 teaspoons of salt. Meanwhile, put the oil and garlic into a deep sauté or frying pan and place it over a medium heat. As soon as the garlic begins to sizzle round the edges, add the crushed chillies, green chilli and sliced porcini and cook briskly for 2–3 minutes. Add the tomatoes and cook for a further minute or two. Set to one side and keep hot.

Step two Add the pasta to the pan of boiling water and cook for 9 minutes or until al dente. Heat another large pan over a high heat. Add the clams and the wine, cover and cook over a high heat for 2–3 minutes until they have all just opened. (Discard any that stay closed.) Tip them into a colander set over a bowl to collect the clam juices.

Step three Add all but the last tablespoon or two of the clam cooking liquor (which might be gritty) to the porcini sauce, return to the heat and simmer rapidly until it has reduced by half to a well-flavoured sauce.

Step four Drain the pasta and return to the pan with the cooked clams, the porcini sauce and parsley and toss together well. Serve immediately.

Serves 4

5 tbsp extra-virgin olive oil

4 garlic cloves, thinly sliced

¼ tsp crushed dried chillies

1 mild green chilli, stalk removed and thinly sliced

225g (8oz) fresh porcini mushrooms, cleaned and thickly sliced

2 large, ripe vine tomatoes, skinned, deseeded and sliced

400 g (14oz) dried spaghetti

1 kg (2lb 4oz) small clams, such as carpet-shell, washed

60ml (2fl oz) dry white wine

a large handful of finely chopped flat-leaf parsley

Pearl Barley Risotto with Mussels and Lobster

Here I've used the shell of a lobster to flavour the stock and then added the meat at the end, and the result is something quite special.

Serves 4

50g (2oz) butter

1 onion, chopped

2 garlic cloves, chopped

300g (11oz) pearl barley

150ml (¼ pint) dry white wine

20 mussels, cleaned

1 large vine-ripened tomato, skinned, deseeded and diced

freshly chopped flat-leaf parsley, to garnish

for the broth

1 x 450g (1lb) cooked lobster

4 tbsp olive oil

1 onion, chopped

25g (1oz) garlic cloves, thinly sliced

1 fennel head, sliced

1 red pepper, deseeded and chopped

4 pitted black olives, roughly chopped

large pinch crushed dried chillies

120ml (4fl oz) dry white wine

1kg (2lb 4oz) gurnard, cut across into slices

pinch of saffron strands

2 tbsp tomato purée

Step one To make the broth, cut the lobster in half and remove the meat from the claws and the tail. Cut the tail meat across into slices, place in a bowl with the claw meat, cover and set aside. Cut up the lobster shells into chunky pieces. Heat the oil in a large pan, add the onion and garlic, and fry over a medium-high heat until lightly browned. Add the fennel, red pepper, black olives, crushed dried chillies and wine, and fry for a further 10 minutes. Add the lobster shells, gurnard, saffron, tomato purée and 2 litres water and leave to simmer gently, uncovered, for 45 minutes.

Step two When the broth is ready, crush everything down into the stock with a potato masher to release as much flavour as possible from the ingredients. Then pass through a fine sieve into a clean pan, bring back to the boil and reduce to 1.2 litres (2 pints). Add 1 teaspoon of salt and keep the broth hot.

Step three For the risotto, melt the butter in a medium-sized pan, add the onion and garlic and cook gently until soft but not browned. Add the pearl barley and cook for 2 minutes, stirring, then add the wine and simmer, stirring, until the wine has almost disappeared. Add a ladleful of the hot seafood stock and stir over a medium heat until it has been absorbed before adding another. Continue like this for about 40 minutes until the pearl barley is cooked but still a little al dente. You might not need to use all the stock.

Step four As you come to add the last ladleful of stock, stir in the mussels, diced tomato and lobster meat and continue to cook for about 3 minutes until the mussels have opened and the lobster meat has heated through. Season to taste and serve immediately in warmed bowls, sprinkled with chopped parsley.

Chicken and Prawn Paella with Artichokes and Chorizo

This is a great dish for a big group of people.

Step one Joint the chicken and remove the bones from the breasts and thighs. Cut the knuckle end off each drumstick and leave the wings as they are. Cut the breast and thigh meat into large chunks. You could ask your butcher to do this for you.

Step two Put the stock into a large pan, add the chicken bones and leave to simmer for 20 minutes. Strain into a clean pan, add the saffron strands and keep hot.

Step three Heat 4 tablespoons of the oil in a 40cm (16in) paella pan over a medium-high heat, add the chicken and fry until golden brown. Remove the chicken and set aside on a plate. Add another 2 tablespoons of oil to the pan along with half the garlic, the prawns and chorizo sausage, and fry for 1 minute until lightly golden. Set aside on another plate.

Step four Add the onions, the remaining oil (4 tablespoons) and garlic to the pan and cook for 5 minutes until lightly golden. Add the tomatoes and leave to cook over a low heat for 15 minutes until you have a jam-like consistency. Add the rice to the pan, turn up the heat and fry for 1–2 minutes. Then add the stock, the chicken, the artichokes, rosemary and 2 teaspoons of salt and stir. Leave to simmer for 20 minutes, turning the pan now and then so that it cooks evenly.

Step five Meanwhile, drop the green beans into a pan of boiling salted water and cook for 3 minutes. Drain and refresh under cold water. Scatter the beans, peas, prawns and chorizo over the top of the rice and cook for a further 10 minutes, by which time the rice should have absorbed all the stock and be tender, and all the other ingredients should be cooked. Leave the paella to rest off the heat for 5 minutes.

Serves 10–12

1 x 1.5kg (3lb) chicken

1.75 litres (3 pints) good-quality chicken stock

½ tsp loosely packed saffron strands

150ml (¼ pint) olive oil

8 garlic cloves, sliced

16 large raw prawns, heads removed but left unpeeled

150g (5oz) chorizo picante, sliced

2 onions, chopped

2 beef tomatoes, skinned and chopped

750g (1lb 10oz) arroz calasparra (paella rice)

300g (11oz) prepared artichoke hearts

leaves from 10cm (4in) rosemary sprig

150g (5oz) fine green beans, trimmed and cut into 1.5cm (¾in) pieces

150g (5oz) fresh peas

Spaghettini with Anchovies, Parsley and Crisp Breadcrumbs

This classic Sicilian recipe is a celebration of anchovies.

Serves 4

for the breadcrumbs

4 fat garlic cloves, peeled

6 tbsp extra-virgin olive oil

225g (8oz) white breadcrumbs, made from day-old white bread

8 anchovy fillets in olive oil, drained

4 tbsp freshly chopped flat-leaf parsley

for the sauce

2 tbsp tomato purée

5 tbsp olive oil

3 garlic cloves, finely chopped

10 anchovy fillets in olive oil, drained

400g (14oz) dried spaghettini

Step one For the breadcrumbs, lightly crush the garlic under the blade of a large knife. Put the crushed cloves into a large frying pan with 5 tablespoons of the oil and place the pan over a medium heat. Fry the garlic until it just starts to colour, then remove and discard. Add the breadcrumbs to the oil and fry over a medium heat, stirring constantly, for about 5 minutes until crisp and golden. Spoon onto a plate and wipe the pan clean.

Step two Chop the anchovy fillets. Add the remaining tablespoon of oil to the pan, add the chopped anchovies and cook over a low heat, breaking them up a little with a wooden spoon, until they have dissolved into the oil. Return the breadcrumbs to the pan along with the parsley and a little seasoning, and stir well. Set aside and keep warm.

Step three To make the sauce, mix the tomato purée with 2 tablespoons of hot water until smooth. Put the oil and garlic into a frying pan and place over a medium heat. As soon as the garlic begins to sizzle, add the tomato purée, anchovies and 175ml (6fl oz) water and leave to simmer gently for 10 minutes.

Step four Meanwhile, bring 4.5 litres (7½ pints) water to the boil in a large pan with 8 teaspoons of salt. Add the spaghettini and cook for 5–6 minutes or until al dente. Drain well, return to the pan, add the sauce and toss together well. Divide the spaghettini between four warmed serving bowls and sprinkle with some of the anchovy breadcrumbs. Serve the rest of the breadcrumbs separately.

Seafood Couscous

I visited the Tonnara di Bonagia, just outside Trapani, in Sicily, when filming *Mediterranean Escapes*. The thing about the couscous we ate there was that it was so simple. Just an excellent seafood broth stirred into mounds of steamed couscous flavoured with bay and nutmeg.

Step one To make the stock, heat the oil in a large pan over a medium heat. Add the onion and garlic and sweat gently for 5–6 minutes until soft. Add the nutmeg, passata, 2 litres (3½ pints) water, 2 teaspoons salt and ½ teaspoon white pepper. Bring to the boil, add the fish and simmer, part-covered, for 2 hours. Strain the stock through a fine sieve into a clean pan, pressing out as much of the liquid as you can with the back of a ladle, and set aside. Discard what's left in the sieve.

Step two For the couscous, preheat the oven to 150°C/300°F/ gas 2. Bring 500ml (18fl oz) water, 2 tablespoons of the oil, the bay leaves and 1 teaspoon salt to the boil in a large pan. Stir in the couscous, cover and set aside for 2 minutes. Uncover and separate the grains with a fork (or your fingers). Heat the remaining olive oil in a large flameproof casserole, add the onion and cook gently for 5–6 minutes until soft and very lightly golden. Add the couscous, nutmeg, parsley, ½ teaspoon salt and 1 teaspoon white pepper. Stir well, cover and place in the oven for 15 minutes.

Step three Shortly before serving, bring the seafood broth back up to the boil, then reduce the heat and keep hot. Heat the 2–3 tablespoons of olive oil in a frying pan. Season the prawns well with salt and pepper, add to the pan and fry for 2 minutes until lightly browned and cooked through.

Step four Stir 450ml (¾ pint) of the hot broth through the couscous and spoon it onto one large serving dish or six warmed plates, and scatter the prawns on top. Pour some more of the seafood broth into a jug and serve alongside the couscous.

Serves 6

2–3 tbsp olive oil

24 large raw, unpeeled prawns

for the stock

80ml (3fl oz) olive oil

1 large onion, sliced

4 garlic cloves, chopped

¼ tsp freshly grated nutmeg

500ml (18fl oz) tomato passata

1.5kg (3lb) mixed fish such as gurnard, whiting, grey mullet and conger eel, cut into thick slices

salt and ground white pepper

for the couscous

5 tbsp olive oil

3 fresh bay leaves

500g (1lb) quick-cook couscous

1 large onion, finely chopped

½ tsp freshly grated nutmeg

2 tbsp freshly chopped flat-leaf parsley

Tortilla of Salt Cod with Sweet Onions and Potatoes

All fish from the cod family, such as haddock, hake, pollack or coley, are pleasant to eat when salted. I think the cheaper the fish, the more appropriate it is for salting. Pollack, for example, is much better salted than as a fresh fish.

Serves 6

350g (12 oz) fresh salt cod, soaked (see page 35 for soaking method)

85ml (3fl oz) extra-virgin olive oil

1 large onion, thinly sliced

450g (1lb) potatoes, peeled and cut into chunky matchsticks

8 eggs

3 tbsp freshly chopped flat-leaf parsley

Step one Drop the prepared salt cod into a pan of boiling water and simmer for 6–8 minutes or until just cooked. Lift out and, when cool enough to handle, break the fish into large flakes, discarding the skin and any bones.

Step two Heat the oil in a deep 23cm (9in) well-seasoned or non-stick frying pan. Add the onion and cook over a medium heat for 3–4 minutes. Add the potatoes and cook, stirring now and then, for 15 minutes or until just tender. Add the flaked fish and a little seasoning and turn everything over once or twice to distribute the ingredients evenly. Beat the eggs with the parsley and a little salt and pepper. Pour them into the pan and cook over a very low heat for about 15 minutes, until almost set.

Step three Preheat the grill to high. Put the pan under the grill for 2–3 minutes, until the tortilla is lightly browned on top. Cut it into wedges and serve warm.

Moules Marinière with Cream, Garlic and Parsley

I stumbled across a poem in *The Nation's Favourite Poems of Desire*, in which Elizabeth Garrett subtly described the sensuality of eating mussels with your fingers. Her description of cooking the mussels – 'I pour on wine; it seems they beg for more' – seems very appropriate for the following recipe!

Step one Soften the garlic and shallots in the butter with the bouquet garni, in a large pan big enough to take all the mussels – it should only be half full. Add the mussels and wine, turn up the heat, then cover and steam them for 3–4 minutes, giving the pan a good shake every now and then, until all have just opened. Discard any mussels that have not opened.

Step two Remove the bouquet garni, add the cream and parsley and remove from the heat. Spoon into four large warmed bowls and serve with lots of crusty bread.

Serves 4

1 garlic clove, finely chopped

2 shallots, finely chopped

15g (½ oz) butter

a bouquet garni of parsley, thyme and bay leaves

1.75kg (4lb) mussels, cleaned

100ml (3½ fl oz) dry white wine

120ml (4fl oz) double cream

a handful of parsley leaves, coarsely chopped

crusty bread, to serve

For a video masterclass on cleaning mussels go to
www.mykitchentable.co.uk/videos/cleaningmussels

Coconut Chilli Prawns with Cumin Puris

The combination of chilli, coconut and coriander is what I would call the holy trinity of Indian fish cookery. The added pleasure here are the cumin puris, which are freshly made using wholemeal flour flavoured with cumin seeds.

Serves 4

3 tbsp sunflower oil

2½ cm (1in) piece of fresh root ginger, finely grated

3 garlic cloves, crushed

2 tbsp ready-made rogan josh or Goan masala paste (see page 76)

450g (1lb) large raw prawns, peeled

50g (2oz) creamed coconut, chopped

150ml (¼ pint) hot water

2 tbsp chopped coriander

2 red bird's eye chillies, deseeded and very finely chopped

2 spring onions, sliced

for the cumin puris

100g (4oz) wholemeal flour

100g (4oz) plain flour

½ tsp salt

2 tbsp sunflower oil, plus extra for brushing

1 tsp cumin seeds

150ml (¼ pint) water

Step one First make the puris: sift the flours and salt into a large bowl, add the oil and rub it into the flour with your fingertips until well mixed in. Stir in the cumin seeds. Gradually mix in the water to make a soft, slightly sticky dough, then turn out onto a well-floured work surface and knead for 5 minutes. Rub the ball of dough with a little more oil, put it in a clean bowl, cover and leave for 30 minutes.

Step two Preheat the grill to high. Knead the dough again for about 3 minutes, until smooth. Divide into 12 balls, dust them quite heavily with flour and then roll out into 12½cm (5in) discs. Brush them on both sides with oil and grill for 1 minute on each side.

Step three To cook the prawns, heat the 3 tablespoons of oil in a large pan, add the ginger and garlic and fry for 30 seconds. Add the rogan josh or Goan masala paste and fry for 2 minutes, until it looks as if it is splitting away from the oil. Add the prawns to the pan and stir-fry over a high heat for 3 minutes, until firm and pink. Add the creamed coconut and hot water and stir occasionally until the coconut has melted. Simmer for 1 minute.

Step four Mix the coriander with the chillies and spring onions. Stir into the prawns and serve immediately, with the cumin puris.

Swordfish Steaks with Salmoriglio

The combination of lemon juice, peppery olive oil, garlic and oregano here is all you need. Tuna would make a good alternative fish but, if using, it's imperative to undercook it – about 45°C/115°F in the centre is perfect.

Step one If you are using a charcoal barbecue, light it 40 minutes before you want to start cooking. If you are using a gas barbecue, light it 10 minutes beforehand. If you are using a ridged cast-iron griddle, leave it over a high heat for a couple of minutes until smoking hot, then reduce the heat to medium-high.

Step two Shortly before cooking the fish, make the salmoriglio. Whisk the olive oil and water together in a bowl until thick and creamy then whisk in the lemon juice and some salt to taste. Stir in the garlic, oregano, celery herb, if using, and parsley.

Step three Brush the swordfish generously with olive oil and season well with salt, peperoncino or crushed dried chillies and black pepper. Cook over a medium-high heat for 4 minutes on each side. Serve with the salmoriglio.

Serves 4

4 x 200–225g (7–8oz) swordfish steaks, about 2cm (¾in) thick

a little olive oil

peperoncino or crushed dried chillies

for the salmoriglio

6 tbsp extra-virgin olive oil

3 tbsp water

1½ tbsp fresh lemon juice

1 garlic clove, very finely chopped

1 tbsp chopped oregano

1 tbsp chopped celery herb or celery tops (optional)

1 tbsp freshly chopped flat-leaf parsley

Fillets of John Dory with Cucumber and Noilly Prat

I've done lots of experiments with white wines for fish sauces and I've come to the conclusion that Noilly Prat is the best. The Provençal herbs and spices used to flavour Noilly Prat seem to add flavour to the reduction, and I've done my best here to create a simple homage to sauce vin blanc.

Serves 4

1 cucumber

25g (1oz) butter

4 x 450g (1lb) or 2 x 750–900g (1lb10oz–2lb) John Dory, filleted

for the sauce

600ml (1pint) good-quality fish stock

150ml (¼ pint) Noilly Prat

50ml (2fl oz) double cream

20g (¾oz) chilled butter, cut into small pieces

1 tbsp finely shredded basil

Step one First make the sauce. Put the fish stock and Noilly Prat into a pan and boil rapidly until reduced by three-quarters to about 180ml (6fl oz). Now add the cream and continue to boil for 2 minutes. Remove from the heat and set aside.

Step two Peel the cucumber and then cut in half lengthways. Scoop out the seeds with a melon baller or teaspoon and then cut each half across into slices 1cm (½in) thick.

Step three Preheat the grill to high. Melt the butter for the fish in a large heavy-based frying pan. Brush the fish with a little of the butter, season on both sides with salt and a little ground pepper. Place skin-side up on a lightly greased baking sheet and set aside.

Step four Heat the remaining melted butter until foaming, add the prepared cucumber and cook over a high heat for 1–2 minutes, shaking the pan every now and then, until lightly coloured. Season with salt and a little ground white pepper and remove from the heat.

Step five Grill the fillets of John Dory: 2–3 minutes for those from the smaller fish, 5 minutes for those from the larger, until the skin is lightly browned and the fish is just cooked through. Bring the sauce back to the boil and whisk in the butter, a few pieces at a time. Season to taste with a little salt.

Step six To serve, place the John Dory fillets on four warm plates, spoon the cucumber alongside the fish and sprinkle with the basil. Spoon the sauce around the edge of the plates, and serve.

Monkfish with Saffron and Roasted Red Pepper Dressing

The idea of mixing what is basically a vinaigrette with a wine and fish stock reduction and some butter isn't original, but nevertheless it's still a really good dressing for fish. As I like to say, 'It should taste tart but not too tart, salty but not too salty and generally round and pleasing'.

Step one To prepare the roasted red pepper dressing, put the fish stock, vermouth and saffron into a small pan and simmer until reduced by three-quarters, then set aside. Meanwhile, peel and deseed the peppers and finely chop the flesh. Mix together the extra-virgin olive oil and vinegar with some salt and pepper.

Step two If you are using a charcoal barbecue, light it 30 minutes before you want to cook. If you are using a gas barbecue, light it 10 minutes beforehand. You could also use a ridged cast iron griddle if you wish. Mix the olive oil with the thyme and some salt and pepper. Brush it over the monkfish fillets and cook them on the barbecue or griddle for 10 minutes, turning them until cooked through. Lift onto a plate and keep warm.

Step three To finish the dressing, return the reduced fish stock to the heat and add the chopped red peppers and the vinegar dressing and bring to a brisk boil. Once it has taken on a concentrated flavour, whisk in the butter to give the sauce a light amalgamation. Remove from the heat.

Step four Mix the salad leaves with lemon olive oil and some salt and place on four plates. Slice each monkfish fillet on the diagonal into four thick pieces so that they fall against each other pleasingly. Place each sliced fillet on top of the leaves and pour the roasted red pepper dressing around it. Serve immediately.

To make lemon olive oil, pare the zest from 1 lemon with a potato peeler. Cut the zest into thin strips and mix with 600ml (1 pint) of extra virgin olive oil. Leave to infuse for 24 hours before using.

Serves 4

2 tbsp olive oil

1 tbsp finely chopped thyme

4 monkfish fillets, each weighing about 200g (7oz)

1.2 litre (2 pint) measuring jug loosely filled with salad leaves

1 tbsp lemon olive oil (see left)

for the roasted red pepper dressing

600ml (1 pint) good-quality fish stock

85ml (3fl oz) dry vermouth

a large pinch of saffron

2 roasted red peppers (see page 88)

85ml (3fl oz) extra-virgin olive oil

1 tbsp balsamic vinegar or sherry vinegar

1 tsp unsalted butter

Grilled Red Mullet with an Aubergine and Pesto Salad

What could be better than red mullet fillets with some grilled aubergines, pesto and salad? It is a perfect combination of flavours. This dish has its roots in the cooking of Simon Hopkinson, who used to be the chef at Bibendum restaurant in London.

Serves 4

½ aubergine

olive oil, for brushing

4 red mullet fillets, each weighing about 75–100g (3–4oz)

for the pesto

15g (½ oz) fresh basil

2 large garlic cloves

175ml (6fl oz) olive oil

15g (½ oz) Parmesan cheese, finely grated

15g (½ oz) pine nuts

for the salad

75g (3oz) mixed salad leaves

1 tomato, skinned, deseeded and chopped

1 tsp lemon olive oil (see page 143)

Step one Put all the pesto ingredients in a liquidiser, blend for about 10 seconds and then remove half the mixture and set aside; it should be fairly coarse at this stage. Blend the remaining pesto until it is smooth.

Step two Preheat the grill to high. Cut the aubergine into four 1cm (½in) thick slices. Brush liberally with olive oil and season with salt. Grill until just cooked through.

Step three Brush the red mullet fillets with olive oil and season with salt and pepper. Grill for about 2 minutes on each side.

Step four Meanwhile, spread the aubergine slices with the coarse pesto and place under the grill until the pesto has warmed through. Place an aubergine slice on each of four warmed plates and arrange the fish alongside them.

Step five Toss the salad leaves with the tomato, lemon olive oil (or just add a squeeze of lemon juice with your best olive oil) and some salt, and put a small pile on each plate. Pour the smooth pesto around each plate, making sure that some, but not all, trickles over the fillets, and serve immediately.

Have you made this recipe? Tell us what you think at www.mykitchentable.co.uk/blog

KITCHEN TABLE

144

Roasted Skate Wings with Chilli Beans

Technically, this is a recipe for ray rather than skate. Sadly, skate is now seriously depleted. So why do I call it skate? Because it sounds better and is a name people are familiar with.

Step one Drain the cannellini beans and put them into a pan with fresh water to cover. Bring to the boil, skimming off any scum as it rises to the surface. Cover and simmer for 1 hour or until just tender. Drain and set aside.

Step two Preheat the oven to 200°C/400°F/gas 6. Dry the skate wings with kitchen paper and then sprinkle on both sides with the paprika and coarsely crushed black pepper.

Step three For the chilli beans, put the olive oil, garlic and red chillies in a pan over a medium heat. As soon as the garlic and chillies start to sizzle, add the onion and cook for 5 minutes until soft. Add the cooked beans and 300ml (10fl oz) of the stock and leave them to simmer for 10 minutes.

Step four To cook the skate wings, melt the butter in a roasting tin on top of the stove. Add the wings and lightly brown them for 1 minute on each side. Sprinkle with a little salt, transfer to the oven and roast for 10 minutes.

Step five Meanwhile, stir the tomatoes into the beans and simmer for a further 10 minutes. Stir in the tarragon and season to taste with salt and pepper.

Step six To serve, spoon some of the beans onto the centres of four warmed plates and put one of the roasted skate wings on top. Place the roasting tin over a moderate heat, add the sherry vinegar and the rest of the chicken stock and leave it to boil for a minute or two, scraping up all the crusty bits from the bottom of the tin. Strain the sauce through a fine sieve into a small pan, season to taste and then spoon over the top of the skate.

Serves 4

4 x 225g (8oz) prepared skate wings

1 tsp paprika

1 tsp coarsely crushed black peppercorns

50g (2oz) butter

3 tbsp sherry vinegar

for the chilli beans

350g (12 oz) dried cannellini beans, soaked in cold water overnight

2 tbsp extra-virgin olive oil

1 garlic clove, finely chopped

2 medium-hot red chillies, deseeded and finely chopped

1 small onion, finely chopped

350ml (12fl oz) good-quality chicken stock

2 beef tomatoes, skinned, deseeded and diced

1 tsp chopped tarragon

Skewers of Squid Cooked over Charcoal with an Oregano and Hot Red Pepper Dressing

Squid is the perfect seafood for cooking on the barbecue, as the smoky flavour from the coals is so good with it. I've scored the squid into a diamond-shaped pattern that makes it curl attractively, and the skewers are essential to stop the pieces falling through the bars. The warm potatoes, the spring onions and the slightly peppery red wine vinegar dressing are all you need in addition.

Serves 4

2 medium-sized squid (about 600g/1lb 5oz), cleaned

a generous pinch of crushed dried chillies

450g (1lb) firm, yellow-fleshed new potatoes, peeled, scrubbed or scraped clean

1½ tbsp red wine vinegar

5 tbsp extra-virgin olive oil, plus extra for brushing

1 tsp dried oregano

pinch of Aleppo pepper or cayenne pepper

4 spring onions, trimmed and thinly sliced

Step one If you're using a charcoal barbecue, light it 40 minutes before you want to start cooking. If you are using a gas barbecue, light it 10 minutes beforehand.

Step two Cut the body pouch of each squid open along one side and score the inner side with the tip of a small, sharp knife into a fine diamond pattern. Cut each pouch lengthways into three strips and then each one across into three even-sized pieces. Separate each set of tentacles into pairs. Roll up each piece of squid, scored-side outermost, and thread four pieces of squid and a couple of tentacle pairs onto four 20cm (8in) long, fine metal skewers. Brush with olive oil, season with salt and pepper, and sprinkle with the crushed dried chillies.

Step three Bring a pan of salted water to the boil. Cut the potatoes across into 4–5mm (¼in) thick slices. Drop the potato slices into the boiling water and cook for 5 minutes, or until just tender. Drain, return to the pan, cover and keep warm.

Step four To make the dressing, whisk together the red wine vinegar and 5 tablespoons olive oil, then stir in the dried oregano, Aleppo or cayenne pepper and ¼ teaspoon salt.

Step five Barbecue the squid for 2 minutes on each side until cooked through. Overlap the potato slices in the centre of four plates, scatter with the spring onions and rest one skewer of squid on top. Spoon over some dressing and serve.

Roasted Fish with a Hot, Sour and Sweet Sauce

Instead of roasting, as in the recipe here, you could also barbecue or grill the fish, or even deep-fry it, as the Thais love to do, at 190°C/375°F for 5–6 minutes until crisp and golden. Whichever method you choose, this dish is very simple and completely delicious. Serve it with steamed pak choy and Thai jasmine rice.

Step one Preheat the oven to 220°C/425°F/gas 7. Make three slashes on either side of each fish and place them in a shallow dish. Pour over the fish sauce and work it into the slashes and the belly cavity. Pour the excess off into a small pan. You should be left with about 50ml (2fl oz) but, if not, make up to this amount. Set the fish to one side while you make the sauce.

Step two Heat 1cm (½in) oil in a medium-sized frying pan over a medium-high heat. Add the sliced shallots and fry them, stirring now and then, until they are crisp and golden. Lift out with a slotted spoon onto kitchen paper and leave to drain. Add the sliced garlic to the oil and fry until crisp and golden. Lift out and leave to cool and drain. Add the sliced chillies and fry for a few seconds until lightly golden. Remove and leave to drain too.

Step three Add the sugar, tamarind pulp and 4 tablespoons water to the small pan containing the fish sauce. Bring to the boil, stirring to break up the tamarind pulp, and simmer for about 1 minute until thickened. Pass through a sieve into a bowl, pressing out as much liquid as you can with a wooden spoon. Return to a clean pan and set aside.

Step four Transfer the fish to a lightly oiled roasting tin and roast for 12 minutes or until the flesh at the thickest part, just behind the head, is opaque and comes away from the bones easily.

Step five Bring the sauce back to a gentle simmer and stir in half the fried shallots, garlic and chilli. Lift the fish onto warmed plates and spoon over some of the sauce. Scatter over the remaining fried shallots, garlic and chilli, and serve.

Serves 4

4 gurnard, farmed sea bass or sea bream, each weighing about 300–400g (11–14oz), scaled and trimmed

75ml (3fl oz) Thai fish sauce, plus extra if needed

vegetable oil, for frying

50g (2oz) shallots, thinly sliced

25g (1oz) garlic, thinly sliced

3 red bird's eye chillies, thinly sliced

50g (2oz) palm sugar

30g (1¼ oz) piece of seedless tamarind pulp

Steamed Monkfish with Wild Garlic and Ginger

Chinese seafood cooking is some of the best in the world. It never ceases to amaze me how rarely one comes into contact with it. Most Chinese restaurants seem to adopt a policy of one menu for Westerners and one for them. Occasionally though, in such restaurants as the Mandarin Kitchen in London, or the restaurant where I had this dish in Glasgow, Ho Wong, they do give you the real thing, and those places are always packed with grateful 'gweilos'.

Serves 2

350–400g (12–14oz) monkfish fillet

½ tbsp very finely shredded fresh root ginger

a small bunch of wild garlic (about 4 leaves), or a small bunch of garlic chives, or 1 garlic clove, snipped or cut into fine shreds

1 tsp sesame oil

1 tbsp dark soy sauce

2 spring onions, thinly sliced on the diagonal

steamed rice, to serve

Step one Lightly season the monkfish fillet with salt and then cut it across into thin slices. Arrange the slices in a single layer over a heatproof serving plate and scatter over the ginger.

Step two Put some sort of trivet in a wide, shallow pan, add 1cm (½in) of water and bring to the boil. Rest the plate on the trivet, cover the pan with a tight-fitting lid and steam for 2–3 minutes, until the fish is almost cooked.

Step three Scatter the wild garlic, garlic chives or shredded fresh garlic over the fish and steam, covered, for a further minute. Meanwhile, put the sesame oil and soy sauce into a small pan and heat briefly.

Step four Remove the fish from the steamer and pour away about half the cooking liquor. Scatter over the spring onions, pour over the hot sesame oil and soy mixture and serve with some steamed rice.

Trout with a Soy, Ginger and Chilli Glaze with Steamed Pak Choy

At the centre of this dish is a very simple process: the reduction of soy sauce and balsamic vinegar, which is then used to coat a just-seared fillet of fish with a deliciously sticky and aromatic glaze. This was the idea of a good chef friend of mine called Leigh Stone-Herbert. He gave me the recipe 12 years ago, and I've been using it ever since.

Step one Blanch the pak choy in lightly salted, boiling water for 3 minutes. Spoon 150ml (¼ pint) of the cooking liquor into a small pan; then drain the pak choy, cover and set aside to keep warm.

Step two Season the trout fillets lightly on both sides with some salt and pepper. Heat the oil in a large frying pan over a high heat. Add the trout fillets and sear them for 30 seconds on each side.

Step three Take the pan off the heat and add the soy sauce, balsamic vinegar, garlic, ginger and chilli. Reduce the heat to medium, return the pan to the heat and cook for 3 minutes, until the trout is just cooked through.

Step four Meanwhile, add the sesame oil, shredded ginger and ¼ teaspoon of salt to the reserved pak choy cooking liquor and slake the cornflour with a tablespoon of cold water. Bring the liquor to the boil, add the cornflour and simmer for 1 minute.

Step five Divide the pak choy between four warmed plates and spoon over some of the sesame- and ginger-flavoured sauce. Rest two of the glazed trout fillets on top and serve garnished with the coriander sprigs, accompanied by steamed rice.

Serves 4

4 x 350g (12 oz) rainbow trout, filleted

2 tbsp sunflower oil

6 tbsp dark soy sauce

4 tbsp balsamic vinegar

1 garlic clove, finely chopped

2½ cm (1in) piece of fresh root ginger, very finely chopped

1 medium-hot red chilli, deseeded and finely chopped

4 fresh coriander sprigs, to garnish

steamed rice, to serve

for the steamed pak choy

450g (1lb) small heads of pak choy, halved lengthways

½ tsp roasted sesame oil

2½ cm (1in) piece of fresh ginger, finely shredded

1 tsp cornflour

Broiled Haddock Fillets with Succotash

The American word 'broiled' simply means grilled. I've kept it in to add the right atmosphere to the dish. You could also use cod, hake or kingfish. American recipes for succotash normally call for lima beans. These are the same as butter beans, one name referring to the capital of Peru, where they were first grown, and the other to their buttery, creamy texture.

Serves 4

175g (6oz) dried butter beans

100g (4oz) rindless smoked streaky bacon, in one piece

1 small onion, chopped

1 tbsp sunflower oil, if needed

300ml (10fl oz) good-quality chicken stock

3 whole corn cobs

50ml (2fl oz) double cream

4 x 175–225g (6–8oz) pieces of unskinned thick haddock fillet

15g (½ oz) butter, melted

2 tbsp snipped fresh chives, plus extra to garnish

Step one Put the dried beans into a pan and cover with plenty of water. Bring to the boil, cover, remove from the heat and leave to soak for 2 hours.

Step two Cut the bacon into 5mm (¼ in) dice, put it into a pan and cook over a low heat until the fat begins to melt. Increase the heat a little and allow it to fry in its own fat until crisp and golden. Add the onion (and the sunflower oil, if it looks a little dry) and cook for about 5 minutes, until soft.

Step three Drain the beans and add them to the pan, along with the stock. Simmer gently until they are just tender and the stock is well reduced. Stand the corn cobs up on a chopping board and slice away all the kernels. Add the corn to the beans, along with the cream, and simmer for 5 minutes.

Step four Meanwhile, preheat the grill to high. Brush the pieces of haddock on both sides with the melted butter and season with salt and pepper. Place, skin side up, on a lightly oiled baking sheet or the rack of the grill pan and grill for 7–8 minutes. Stir the chives into the beans and season with salt and pepper. Spoon the mixture into four warmed soup plates and place the haddock on top. Scatter over a few more chives and serve immediately.

Fried Trout Stuffed with Sliced Ceps, Garlic and Diced Bacon

I made this with fresh ceps while I was in France, but sliced fresh chestnut mushrooms are a very good substitute.

Step one Remove the bones from the fish. To do this, remove the head of each one, and then, working with one fish at a time, start to cut the top fillet away from the bones until you can get the whole blade underneath the fillet. Then rest a hand on top of the fish and cut the rest of the fillet away from the bones until you are about 2.5cm (1in) away from the tail. Turn the fish over and repeat on the other side. Then pull back the top fillet and snip out the backbone, close to the tail, with scissors. The fillets will still be attached at the tail. Repeat with the remaining fish.

Step two Melt the butter in a frying pan and as soon as it is foaming, add the bacon and fry briefly until lightly coloured. Add the ceps and garlic and toss over a medium-high heat for 1 minute until lightly cooked. Season and remove from the heat.

Step three Lay the fish on a chopping board and pull back the top fillet of each one. Season the cut face of the fillets and then cover the bottom fillet with some ceps and bacon mixture. Sprinkle with a little parsley, cover with the top fillet and tie round the whole fish in two places with fine string to hold everything in place.

Step four Season the outside of each fish with a little more salt and pepper, then dredge with the flour and pat off the excess. Heat the oil in one large pan over a moderate heat. Add the fish and fry for 2½ minutes without moving them, until nicely golden. Carefully turn the fish over and cook for another 2½ minutes, until cooked through. Lift the fish onto warmed plates.

Step five Discard the frying oil and wipe the pan clean. Add the butter for the beurre noisette and allow it to melt over a moderate heat. As soon as the butter starts to smell nutty and turns light brown, add the lemon juice, parsley and some seasoning. Pour some of the butter over each fish and serve.

Serves 4

4 trout, each weighing about 300g (11oz)

40g (1½oz) butter

60g (2oz) rindless streaky bacon, chopped

175g (6oz) fresh ceps, trimmed and cut into 4mm (¼in) thick slices

2 garlic cloves, finely chopped

1 tbsp roughly chopped parsley

25g (1oz) plain flour

2 tbsp sunflower oil

for the beurre noisette

75g (3oz) unsalted butter

2 tsp fresh lemon juice

1 heaped tbsp freshly chopped parsley

Hard-fried Fish in Red Curry

Steaks of haddock, hake or salmon or even steaks of monkfish, skinned and cut across the bone, would be a great idea too. You could also try shark or swordfish steaks.

Serves 4

2 tbsp groundnut or sunflower oil, plus extra for deep-frying

3 tbsp Thai red curry paste (see below)

200ml (7fl oz) coconut milk

1 tbsp Thai fish sauce (nam pla)

1 tsp palm sugar or light muscovado sugar

4 x 225g (8oz) John Dory steaks

juice of ½ lime

steamed rice, to serve

Step one Heat the 2 tablespoons of oil in a large, deep frying pan. Add the red curry paste and fry for about 2 minutes, until the paste starts to separate from the oil. Add the coconut milk, fish sauce and sugar and simmer very gently for 10 minutes, until thickened.

Step two Meanwhile, heat some oil for deep-frying to 190°C/ 375°F. Deep-fry the John Dory steaks, two at a time, for 2 minutes until crisp, golden and cooked through. Lift onto a baking sheet lined with kitchen paper and keep warm in a low oven while you cook the rest.

Step three Once the excess oil has drained off the fish, place the steaks onto four warmed serving plates. Stir the lime juice into the sauce along with some seasoning to taste, spoon it over the fish and serve with some steamed rice.

To make Thai red curry paste, roughly chop 5 large medium-hot red chillies, 2½cm (1in) fresh root ginger, 2 lemon grass stalks (remove the outer leaves and tough cores), 6 garlic cloves, 3 small shallots and blend in a food processor with 1 teaspoon each of ground coriander, ground cumin and salt, ¼ teaspoon of blachan (dried shrimp paste), 2 teaspoons of paprika, ½ teaspoon of turmeric powder and 1 tablespoon of sunflower oil to form a smooth paste.

Portuguese Barbecued Sardines with Piri-Piri Oil

This recipe came about as a result of an evening I spent at the Portuguese club in St Helier on the island of Jersey. The Portuguese serve these sardines on thick slices of bread. It's the perfect al fresco dish as, to eat it, you lift the fillets off the bones, eat the fillets and throw away the bones, then eat the bread, which by now is soaked with oil, adding some salad, if you like.

Step one To prepare the sardines, rub off the scales with your thumb, working under cold running water, then gut them and trim off the fins.

Step two To make the piri-piri oil, simply mix all the ingredients together and season with a little salt and pepper. If you are using a charcoal barbecue, light it 30–40 minutes before you want to start cooking. If using a gas barbecue, light it 10 minutes beforehand.

Step three Meanwhile, for the salad, arrange the sliced tomatoes over a large serving plate and sprinkle with the sliced onion and roasted peppers. Season with salt and pepper, scatter over the olives and drizzle with a little oil and vinegar.

Step four When you are ready to cook, the charcoal should be covered in a layer of white ash. Make three shallow slashes on either side of each fish and then brush generously inside and out with the piri-piri oil. Cook them on the barbecue for 3 minutes on each side, until the skin blisters and chars a little bit and the eyes turn opaque. Serve them on the slices of bread with some of the salad to follow.

Serves 4

12–16 fresh sardines

for the piri-piri oil

1 garlic clove, finely chopped

finely grated zest and the juice of 1 small lemon

½ tsp dried chilli flakes

120ml (4fl oz) olive oil

for the salad

4–6 large, vine-ripened tomatoes, thinly sliced

1 red onion, thinly sliced

2 small red peppers, roasted (see page 88) and thinly sliced

50g (2oz) well-flavoured black olives

extra-virgin olive oil

red wine vinegar

crusty bread, thickly sliced, to serve

Barbecued Shrimp with Coleslaw

You can cook this quite successfully under the grill or on a barbecue, but, if using a barbecue, heat the remaining marinade in a small pan to the side of the rack to cook out any raw flavours left from the marinated prawns.

Serves 4

150ml (¼ pint) olive oil

120ml (4fl oz) chilli sauce

3 tbsp Worcestershire sauce

4 garlic cloves, crushed

1 tbsp sweet chilli sauce or clear honey

½ tsp Tabasco sauce

900g (2lb) unpeeled raw prawns

for the coleslaw

325g (12oz) white cabbage, sliced

2 celery sticks, sliced

1 green pepper, sliced

6 spring onions, sliced

3 tbsp chopped dill

2 tsp Dijon mustard

1 heaped tsp creamed horseradish

½ tsp Tabasco sauce

1 tbsp red wine vinegar

2 tbsp extra-virgin olive oil

2 tbsp mayonnaise

pinch of cayenne pepper

Step one Mix together the olive oil, chilli sauce, Worcestershire sauce, garlic, sweet chilli sauce, or honey, and Tabasco sauce in a bowl along with 1 teaspoon of salt. Stir in the prawns, cover and marinate at room temperature for 2 hours, or overnight in the fridge.

Step two Preheat your barbecue or grill. Meanwhile, make the coleslaw: mix together the cabbage, celery, green pepper, spring onions and dill in a bowl. In a separate bowl, mix the rest of the ingredients together to make a dressing. Stir it into the vegetables at the last minute and spoon it into a large serving bowl.

Step three If you are barbecuing the prawns, you might prefer to thread them onto large metal skewers first, which will make things easier when you come to turn them. Cook them for 1½–2 minutes on each side, basting them with some of the marinade. Pile them into a warmed serving bowl. Bring the remaining marinade to the boil in a small pan and pour it over the prawns. Serve them with the coleslaw and plenty of crusty French bread.

Ragoût of Seafood with Lemon and Saffron

You could also use lobster, oysters, langoustines and freshwater crayfish in this recipe.

Step one For the vegetable nage, pare the zest off the piece of lemon and then cut away and discard all the bitter white pith. Cut the flesh across into slices. Roughly chop the vegetables and put them into a pan with the lemon zest and flesh, salt, peppercorns, herbs, fennel seeds and enough water to cover. Bring to the boil and simmer for 20 minutes. Take the pan off the heat and add the wine. Cover and leave to cool for 2 hours.

Step two Strain the nage and pour 1.2 litres (2 pints) into a wide-based pan. (Freeze the rest for later use.) Add the saffron, bring to the boil and boil rapidly until it has reduced to 120ml (4fl oz). Transfer to a small pan and set aside.

Step three Peel the prawns and remove the intestinal tract, leaving the last tail segment in place. Cut each lemon sole fillet diagonally across into four pieces.

Step four Drop the vegetables into a pan of boiling salted water, bring back to the boil, drain and then plunge into cold water to set the colour. Drain once more.

Step five Prepare one stacked or two separate steamers. Put all the blanched vegetables onto one plate and the prawns, lemon sole, mussels and scallops onto another. Steam the vegetables for 3 minutes and the fish for 3–4 minutes. Keep everything warm while you make the sauce.

Step six Drain all the cooking juices from the plate of fish into the reduced stock. Bring back to the boil and then whisk in the butter, a few pieces at a time, until you have a smooth, emulsified sauce. Season to taste with some salt and pepper.

Step seven Arrange the seafood and vegetables on four warmed plates. Spoon over the lemon and saffron sauce and serve sprinkled with some sea salt flakes.

Serves 4

8 unpeeled, large raw prawns

2 x 50–75g (2–3oz) skinned lemon sole fillets

8 baby carrots, scraped and trimmed

8 very small florets of broccoli

8 French beans, trimmed and halved

8 mussels, cleaned

4 prepared scallops

100g (4oz) chilled unsalted butter, diced

sea salt flakes, to garnish

for the vegetable nage

½ lemon

1 fennel head

1 large onion, peeled

4 celery sticks

a handful of button mushrooms

½ tsp salt

1 tsp black peppercorns

2 bay leaves

3 sprigs of thyme

½ tsp fennel seeds

300ml (½ pint) white wine

good pinch of saffron strands

Smoked Haddock and Leek Tart

I can never enthuse enough about smoked haddock. Good smoked haddock is only very lightly cured in salt and therefore doesn't keep for a particularly long time, but when it is good, it is sublime.

Serves 6–8

20g (¾oz) butter

225g (8oz) leeks, thinly sliced

350g (12oz) undyed smoked haddock

a small bunch of chives, snipped

3 large eggs

300ml (½ pint) double cream

15g (½oz) Parmesan cheese, finely grated

for the rich shortcrust pastry

225g (8oz) plain flour

½ tsp salt

65g (2½oz) chilled butter, cut into pieces

65g (2½oz) chilled lard, cut into pieces

1½–2 tbsp cold water

Step one To make the shortcrust pastry, sift the flour and salt into a food-processor or mixing bowl. Add the pieces of chilled butter and lard and work together until the mixture resembles fine breadcrumbs. Stir in the water with a round-bladed knife until the mixture comes together into a ball, then turn out onto a lightly floured work surface and knead briefly until smooth.

Step two Roll out the pastry thinly on a little more flour and use to line a 4cm (1½in) deep, loose-bottomed 25cm (10in) flan tin. Prick the base here and there with a fork and chill for 20 minutes.

Step three Meanwhile, melt the butter in a large pan, add the leeks and some seasoning and cook gently, uncovered, for 15 minutes stirring every now and then, until the leeks are very tender.

Step four Preheat the oven to 200°C/400°F/gas 6. Bring some water to the boil in a large shallow pan. Add the smoked haddock and simmer for 4 minutes, until the fish is just cooked. Lift the fish out onto a plate and leave until cool enough to handle. Then break it into flakes, discarding any skin and bones.

Step five Line the pastry case with greaseproof paper and baking beans then bake blind for 15 minutes. Remove the paper and beans and then return to the oven for 5 minutes, until lightly golden.

Step six Reduce the oven temperature to 190°C/375°F/gas 5. Stir half the chopped chives into the leeks and spoon them over the base of the pastry case. Toss the rest of the chives through the flaked smoked haddock and scatter it over the top. (This helps to stop all the chives from floating to the top during cooking.) Beat the eggs with the cream, Parmesan and some seasoning and pour over the leeks and smoked haddock. Bake for 30–35 minutes, until just set and lightly browned on top. Remove from the oven and leave to cool slightly before serving.

Haddock and Cornish Yarg Pie

If you can't get Cornish Yarg, use a mild Cheddar.

Step one Cook the potatoes in boiling, salted water until tender. Drain well and mash. Put the milk and fish stock into a large pan and bring to the boil. Add the haddock and simmer for 5–7 minutes, until firm and opaque. Lift the fish out onto a plate and break the flesh into large flakes, discarding any skin and bones.

Step two Finely dice 50g (2oz) of the leeks and slice the rest. Melt 25g (1oz) of the butter in a pan, add the sliced leeks and fry for 2–3 minutes, until just cooked. Lift out with a slotted spoon.

Step three Add the diced leek, carrot, celery, onion and bacon to the pan with a little more butter. Fry gently for 10 minutes without letting them brown. Add the remaining butter to the vegetables, stir in the flour and cook for 1 minute. Remove the pan from the heat and gradually add the haddock cooking liquid, stirring constantly to make a smooth sauce. Bring to the boil, stirring. Make the bouquet garni and add to the pan. Simmer for 30 minutes, then discard the bouquet garni. Season with nutmeg.

Step four Stir the fish, reserved leeks, prawns and Cornish Yarg into the sauce, spoon into a deep 1.75-litre (3-pint) pie dish and push a pie funnel into the centre of the mixture. For the pastry, sift the flour and salt into a bowl. Dice the butter and rub it in with your fingertips until the mixture looks like breadcrumbs. Add the potato then the water and stir with a round-bladed knife until everything sticks together. Form it into a ball, turn out onto a floured work surface and knead until smooth. Chill for 20–30 minutes.

Step five Preheat the oven to 200°C/400°F/gas 6. Roll out the pastry until it is slightly larger than the pie dish. Cut a strip off the edge, brush with a little water and press it onto the rim of the pie dish. Brush with a little more water. Make a cut in the centre of the remaining pastry and then lay it over the pie so that the pie funnel pokes through the cut. Press the pastry onto the rim of the dish. Brush the top with beaten egg. Bake in the oven for 35–40 minutes, until the pastry is crisp and golden.

Serves 6

600ml (1 pint) milk

300ml (½ pint) good-quality fish stock

750g (1lb 10oz) haddock fillet

275g (10oz) leeks

65g (2½ oz) butter

50g (2oz) each of carrot and celery, finely diced

50g (2oz) onion, chopped

40g (1½ oz) smoked streaky bacon, sliced

50g (2oz) plain flour

freshly grated nutmeg

100g (4oz) cooked, peeled prawns

100g (4oz) Cornish Yarg cheese, grated

for the bouquet garni

1 bay leaf

a small bunch of parsley, with stalks

leaves from the centre of 1 head of celery

small sprig of thyme

for the potato pastry crust

325g (12oz) floury potatoes, peeled and cut into chunks

225g (8oz) self-raising flour

1 tsp salt

175g (6oz) cold butter

2 tbsp cold water

1 egg, beaten

Grilled Cod with Aïoli and Butter Beans

This is a hot version of the classic Provençal dish, aïoli garni. I would suggest a Côtes de Provence rosé, a Portuguese white Dâo or a white Corbières from south-western France to go with this.

Serves 4

50g (2oz) dried butter beans

2 eggs

1 fennel head

4 fillets of cod, skin on, each weighing about 175–300g (6–7oz)

melted butter, for brushing

4 basil leaves, thinly sliced

1 tsp sea salt

aïoli (see page 42)

for the sauce

225g (8oz) finely chopped mixed carrot, leek, celery and onion

50g (2oz) unsalted butter

1 tbsp Cognac

10g (⅓oz) dried mushrooms

1 tbsp balsamic vinegar

½ medium hot red chilli, deseeded and chopped

2 tbsp olive oil

1 tsp Thai fish sauce

600ml (1 pint) good quality fish stock

½ tsp salt

Step one Bring the butter beans to the boil in a large pan of salted water. Simmer gently until very soft. Remove from the heat and keep warm in the cooking liquid.

Step two To make the sauce, sweat the mixture of carrot, leek, celery and onion in a large pan with half the butter, until soft. Add the Cognac and let it boil. Then add all the rest of the sauce ingredients, except the remaining butter. Simmer for 30 minutes. Then pass the sauce through a fine sieve, bring it back to the boil and simmer until reduced to about 150ml (¼ pint).

Step three Boil the eggs for 7 minutes. Drain, remove the shells and keep warm. Remove the outer leaves of the fennel but don't cut off the tops. Slice into thin sections then cook in salted water until just tender. Drain and keep warm.

Step four Preheat the grill to high. Brush the pieces of cod on both sides with melted butter and place, skin side up, on a greased baking sheet or the rack of the grill pan. Grill for 8 minutes or until just cooked through (this will depend on the thickness of the fillets). Place the cod on four warmed plates. Drain the butter beans and divide between the plates. Add the fennel, then cut the eggs in half and put one half on each plate. Add a spoonful of aïoli to each serving.

Step five Bring the sauce to the boil and whisk in the last 25g (1oz) of butter, then add the finely chopped basil leaves. Pour the sauce over the beans and fish and serve.

Prawns Cooked on Skewers with a Split Tomato, Saffron and Currant Sauce

When I first went to Australia in 1966, I expected to find plenty of prawns and I was not disappointed – they're perhaps my fondest memory of those distant but magic times. I do marvel at the quality and universal availability of Australian prawns.

Step one Put the prawns in a shallow dish. Whisk together the olive oil, lemon juice, oregano and dried chilli flakes with ½ teaspoon of salt and some pepper, pour over the prawns and mix to coat. Cover and marinate in the fridge for 1–2 hours.

Step two Meanwhile, make the sauce. Heat the olive oil in a medium-sized pan. Add the onion and garlic and fry gently for 5 minutes until softened. Add the tomatoes, saffron, dried chilli and some salt and pepper and simmer gently for 15–20 minutes, stirring now and then. Put the sugar and vinegar into a small pan and boil until reduced to 1 teaspoon. Stir into the tomato sauce and adjust the seasoning to taste. Blend the sauce briefly until smooth and then pass through a sieve into a clean pan, add the currants and leave to simmer gently until it is thick enough to coat the back of a spoon. Set aside.

Step three Reheat the sauce. Put the ingredients for the dressing into a bowl with ½ teaspoon of salt and some black pepper and whisk together. Stir into the tomato sauce and keep warm.

Step four Thread the prawns onto skewers. (If using wooden skewers, soak them in cold water first to prevent them from burning on the barbecue.) Barbecue the prawns for 1½ minutes on each side or until cooked through.

Step five To serve, spoon some of the sauce over the base of four warmed plates. Pull the prawns off each set of skewers, arrange on top of the sauce and serve immediately, with finger bowls. Alternatively, spoon the sauce into small bowls and put onto plates, with the prawns piled alongside.

Serves 6

36 large, raw, shell-on prawns

4 tbsp extra-virgin olive oil

juice of ½ lemon

1 tsp dried oregano

1 tsp dried chilli flakes

for the tomato sauce

1 tbsp extra-virgin olive oil

1 small onion, finely chopped

2 garlic cloves, finely chopped

200g (7oz) tinned plum tomatoes

pinch of saffron strands

pinch of dried chilli flakes

1 tsp sugar

2 tbsp red wine vinegar

15g (½ oz) currants

for the dressing

125ml (4fl oz) extra-virgin olive oil

2 tbsp red wine vinegar

Stew of Mussels and Clams Scattered over Chargrilled Bread

I came across this one in a little Sardinian fishing village called Portixeddu. The restaurant was called L'Ancora and it looked just about OK from the outside. But whereas in Britain if you go into a very ordinary-looking place all you'll get is maybe a cup of tea and some baked beans and chips, in Sardinia you can end up with some great food like this.

Serves 4

3 tbsp extra-virgin olive oil, plus extra for drizzling

5 fat garlic cloves, 4 finely chopped and 1 left whole

pinch of peperoncino or crushed dried chillies

1 x 400g tin chopped tomatoes

3 tbsp red wine vinegar

2 tsp caster sugar

500g (1lb) mussels, cleaned

500g (1lb) clams, washed

50ml (2fl oz) dry white wine

4 large slices rustic white bread, taken from a large round loaf

3 tbsp freshly chopped flat-leaf parsley

Step one Put the olive oil, chopped garlic and peperoncino into a large flameproof casserole and place it over a medium heat. As soon as it begins to sizzle, add the tomatoes and 150ml (¼ pint) water and leave to simmer gently for 10 minutes until reduced and thickened. Meanwhile, put the vinegar and sugar into a small pan and boil until reduced to 1 teaspoon. Stir into the tomato sauce and keep hot.

Step two Place another large pan over a high heat and, when hot, add the mussels, clams and white wine, cover and cook for 2–3 minutes until the shellfish have just opened. Tip the mussels, clams and all but the last tablespoon or two of the cooking juices (which might be a bit gritty) into the tomato sauce, discarding any mussels or clams that have not opened, and stir well.

Step three Toast the slices of bread on both sides and then singe over a naked gas flame for a slightly smoky taste. Rub one side of each slice of toast with the peeled garlic clove, put the slices of toast into the base of four warmed bistro-style plates and drizzle with a little olive oil. Stir the parsley into the stew, spoon the stew on top of the bread and serve immediately.

For a video masterclass on cleaning mussels go to
www.mykitchentable.co.uk/videos/cleaningmussels

KITCHEN TABLE

Grilled Scallops with a Pumpkin Seed, Serrano Chilli and Coriander Sauce

I've had a lot of success serving scallops grilled in their shells; I think the aroma of hot shells adds a lot of excitement. I've never had a dish like this in Mexico, but I'd love to. Using pumpkin seeds to thicken a sauce or a dressing is very popular there, as is the combination of green chilli and coriander.

Step one For the sauce, put the pumpkin seeds, chilli, coriander, garlic, oil, lime juice, spring onions, Parmesan cheese and ½ teaspoon of salt into a food-processor and blend to a smooth paste.

Step two Preheat the grill to high. Put the scallops onto a baking sheet, brush each one generously with melted butter and season with salt and pepper. Grill the king scallops for 2 minutes or queen scallops for 1 minute.

Step three Lightly spread about 1 teaspoon of the pumpkin-seed sauce over the scallops (use about ½ teaspoon for the 'queenies') and grill for a further 1–2 minutes (1 minute for the queenies) until they are just cooked through and the sauce has just started to colour. Place on four warmed plates and serve immediately.

Serves 4

50g (2oz) pumpkin seeds

1 serrano (hot green) chilli, chopped

a large handful (about 25g/1oz) of coriander leaves

2 garlic cloves, peeled

150ml (¼ pint) sunflower oil

juice of 1 lime

2 spring onions, chopped

7g (¼ oz) Parmesan cheese, grated

16–20 cleaned king scallops or 32 cleaned queen scallops in the shell

25g (1oz) butter, melted

Baked Sea Bass with Roasted Red Peppers, Tomatoes, Anchovies and Potatoes

To prepare the sea bass yourself, first scale the fish working under cold running water over several sheets of newspaper. Grip the fish by its tail and scrape from tail to head using a fish scaler or blunt, thick-bladed knife. Cut away the dorsal, pelvic and anal fins using a strong pair of kitchen scissors. Slit open the belly of the fish from the anal fin up to the head and pull out the guts. Cut away any remaining pieces of gut with a small knife and wash out the cavity with plenty of cold water.

Serves 4

good pinch of saffron strands

900g (2lb) potatoes, peeled and cut into 1cm (½in) slices

4 plum tomatoes, skinned and cut lengthways into quarters

50g (2oz) anchovy fillets in oil, drained

150ml (¼ pint) good-quality chicken stock

4 red peppers, each one deseeded and cut into 8 chunks

8 garlic cloves, each sliced into three

8 small sprigs of oregano

85ml (3fl oz) olive oil

1.5–1.75kg (3–4 lb) sea bass, striped bass or kingfish, cleaned and trimmed

Step one Preheat the oven to 200°C/400°F/gas 6. Place the saffron in a teacup, pour over 2 tablespoons of hot water and leave to soak.

Step two Put the potatoes in a pan of boiling salted water and boil for 7 minutes. Drain well and arrange them in a narrow strip over the base of a roasting dish large enough to hold the sea bass either lengthways or diagonally. The potatoes should form a bed for the fish, leaving plenty of room on either side for the red peppers.

Step three Scatter the tomatoes and anchovy fillets over the potatoes, then pour over the saffron water and stock. Scatter the pieces of red pepper down either side of the potatoes and sprinkle over the garlic, oregano sprigs and olive oil. Season everything well with salt and pepper and bake for 30 minutes.

Step four Slash the fish 5–6 times down each side and then slash it in the opposite direction on just one side to give an attractive criss-cross pattern. Rub it generously with some olive oil, season well with salt and pepper and then rest it on top of the potatoes.

Step five Return the dish to the oven and bake for a further 35 minutes, until the fish is cooked through. Serve with the roasted vegetables.

Mussel, Cockle and Clam Masala

The sauce for this dish shouldn't be too wet; it's much better if it is quite thick and clinging to the shells. I use three different molluscs here because we get plenty of all of them at my restaurant, but it's nearly as good made with only one. Unusually for curry sauces from southern India, the spices are roasted before being blended and this gives a slightly spicier and less aromatic flavour.

Step one To make the masala paste, heat a dry, heavy-based frying pan over a medium-high heat. Add the coriander seeds, cloves and cumin seeds and cook until they darken slightly and start to smell aromatic. Tip into a spice grinder and grind to a powder. Put this mixture and all the other paste ingredients into a food-processor and blend until smooth.

Step two Heat the oil in a large pan, add the masala paste and fry for a few minutes until it starts to separate from the oil. Add the mussels, cockles and clams, cover and cook over a high heat for 3–4 minutes, shaking the pan now and then, until they have all opened. Discard any that have not opened.

Step three Add a little water if there is not quite enough sauce, season with a little salt if necessary, then add the chopped coriander. Spoon into warmed bowls and serve.

Serves 4

2 tbsp sunflower oil

1.75 kg (4lb) mixed live mussels, cockles and small clams, cleaned

2 tbsp roughly chopped coriander

for the masala paste

1 tbsp coriander seeds

1 tsp cloves

2 tbsp cumin seeds

2 onions, quartered

8 large garlic cloves

50g (2oz) fresh root ginger, chopped

a walnut-sized piece of seedless tamarind pulp

1 tsp ground turmeric

3 medium-hot red chillies, chopped

2 tbsp red wine vinegar

40g (1½oz) creamed coconut

Have you made this recipe? Tell us what you think at
www.mykitchentable.co.uk/blog

Monkfish Vindaloo

I originally used shark in this recipe but of late, sadly, stocks have diminished alarmingly, so we changed to monkfish, which is possibly even better. Serve with pilau rice.

Serves 4

3-4 tbsp groundnut or sunflower oil

1 onion, chopped

2 tomatoes, chopped

300ml (½ pint) water

4 medium-hot green chillies

900g (2lb) skinned monkfish tail, sliced into 2½ cm (1in) steaks

white wine vinegar, to taste

for the vindaloo paste

40g (1½ oz) dried Kashmiri chillies

1 small onion, unpeeled

1 tsp black peppercorns

1½ tsp cloves

7½ cm (3in) cinnamon stick

1 tsp cumin seeds

2½ cm (1in) piece of fresh root ginger

4 tbsp roughly chopped garlic

a walnut-sized piece of tamarind pulp, without seeds

1 tsp light soft brown sugar

2 tbsp white wine vinegar

Step one To make the vindaloo paste, cover the chillies with plenty of hot water and leave them to soak overnight. The next day, preheat the oven to 230°C/450°F/gas 8. Place the unpeeled onion on the middle shelf and roast for 1 hour until the centre is soft and the skin is nicely caramelised. Remove from the oven and leave to cool, then peel off the skin. Drain the chillies, squeeze out the excess water and then roughly chop. Put the peppercorns, cloves, cinnamon and cumin seeds into a mortar or spice grinder and grind to a fine powder. Tip the powder into a mini food-processor and add the roasted onion, chillies, ginger, garlic, tamarind pulp, sugar and vinegar. Blend to a smooth paste.

Step two Heat the oil in a large, deep frying pan. Add the chopped onion and fry until richly browned. Add the tomatoes and cook until they form a deep-golden paste. Stir in 4 tablespoons of the vindaloo paste and fry gently for 5 minutes, stirring, until it has slightly caramelised. Add the water and leave the sauce to simmer for 10 minutes, giving it a stir every now and then.

Step three Meanwhile, slit the green chillies open along their length and scrape out the seeds but leave them whole. Add the monkfish steaks and the chillies to the sauce and simmer for 10 minutes, carefully turning the fish halfway through if necessary. Then lift the steaks out onto a plate and boil the sauce rapidly until reduced to a good consistency. Add some vinegar and salt to taste, return the steaks to the sauce and reheat. Spoon onto four warmed plates and serve with pilau rice.

Singapore Chilli Crab

Prepare the crab for stir-frying by removing the tail flap and claws from the body, discarding the 'dead man's fingers' and back shell and then chopping the body (with legs attached) and each claw into two pieces. Reserve the liquid from the back shell for the sauce. You could also use large raw prawns or uncooked lobster for this recipe.

Step one Heat the oil in a large wok. Add the crab pieces and stir-fry for 3 minutes, adding the garlic and ginger after 1 minute.

Step two Add the juices from the back shell, the tomato ketchup, red chillies, soy sauce, water and black pepper. Cover and simmer over a medium heat for 5 minutes if the crab is fresh, or 2–3 minutes if using cooked crab.

Step three Spoon the crab onto one large plate or four soup plates, sprinkle over the shredded spring onions and serve immediately.

Serves 4

1 tbsp groundnut or sunflower oil

2 x 800g chilli uncooked or cooked crabs

4 large garlic cloves finely chopped

2.5cm (1in) fresh root ginger, finely chopped

4 tbsp tomato ketchup

3 medium-hot red Dutch chillies, finely chopped

2 tbsp dark soy sauce

150ml (¼ pint) water

a few turns of the black pepper mill

2 spring onions, cut into 5cm (2in) pieces and finely shredded lengthways

Sri Lankan Fish Curry

I got this recipe from a Sri Lankan living in Cumbria. Rampe, or screwpine, is a plant of the genus *Pandanus* whose leaves, or an essence extracted from them, are a popular flavouring in South-east Asian cooking, especially desserts and rice dishes. It should be available from Asian food stores.

Serves 4

4 x 225g (8oz) salmon steaks

2 tbsp sunflower oil

1 large onion, chopped

4 garlic cloves, finely chopped

8 fresh curry leaves

2 small pieces **rampe** or screwpine (optional; see above)

½ tsp ground turmeric

1 tsp chilli powder

1 x quantity Sri Lankan curry powder (see right)

3 tomatoes, skinned and chopped

85ml (3fl oz) tamarind water (see page 12)

1 x 400ml tin coconut milk

some steamed rice and mango, lime, aubergine or tamarind chutney, to serve

Step one Rinse the fish steaks under cold water and dry on kitchen paper. Heat the oil in a large, shallow pan, add the onion, garlic, curry leaves and rampe, if using, and fry gently for 7–10 minutes, until the onion is soft and lightly golden.

Step two Add the turmeric, chilli powder and 2 tablespoons of the Sri Lankan curry powder and fry for 1–2 minutes. Add the tomatoes, tamarind water (see page 12), coconut milk and 1 teaspoon of salt and simmer gently for 15 minutes.

Step three Add the salmon steaks to the pan and spoon some of the sauce over them. Simmer gently for 5 minutes, then cover the pan and set aside for 30 minutes. By this time the fish should be cooked through – but if not, just return it to the heat for a few minutes. Serve with steamed rice and mango, lime, aubergine or tamarind chutney.

To make the Sri Lankan curry powder, put 2½ tablespoons of coriander seeds, 1 tablespoon of cumin seeds, 1½ teaspoons of fennel seeds, a pinch of fenugreek seeds, 2½cm (1in) cinnamon stick, 3 cloves, 2 green cardamom pods and 6 black peppercorns into a spice grinder and grind to a fine powder. Store in a screw-top jar.

Squid and Potato Stew with Rouille

This local dish from Sète, is often made with octopus. However, squid is much easier to get hold of in Britain, and if anything it's nicer. This is a hearty seafood stew in the tradition of bouillabaisse (see page 192).

Step one Clean the squid and cut the pouches across into about 1cm (½in) thick rings and the tentacles and wings into similar-sized pieces.

Step two Heat 3 tablespoons of the olive oil in a large, deep frying pan. Add the onion and garlic and fry gently until soft but not browned. Add the Cognac, light it with a match and shake the pan until the flames have died down. Then add the red pepper, tomatoes, tomato purée, orange zest, thyme, bay leaf, star anise, white wine and stock and bring up to a simmer.

Step three Heat another tablespoon of olive oil in a frying pan, add half the squid and a little seasoning and stir-fry over a high heat for 2 minutes until lightly browned. Add to the sauce, cook the remaining squid in the same way and add to the sauce. Season to taste with salt and pepper, part-cover the pan and leave to simmer gently for 1 hour, until the squid is tender and the liquid has reduced and thickened.

Step four Meanwhile, put the potatoes into a pan of well-salted water (1 teaspoon per 600ml/1pint), bring to the boil and simmer for 7–10 minutes until just tender. Drain well and set aside.

Step five When the squid is tender, remove the orange zest and pieces of star anise from the stew, add the potatoes and simmer for 5–10 minutes so that they take on some of the flavours.

Step six Meanwhile, make the rouille according to the instructions on page 7. Take the pan of stew off the heat and add 2 spoonfuls of the liquid from the stew to the rouille. Mix well and stir it back into the pan, but don't put the pan back over the heat or it might curdle. Adjust the seasoning if necessary, sprinkle with parsley and serve with plenty of bread.

Serves 4

750g (1lb 10oz) squid
(pouches, tentacles
and wings)

5 tbsp extra-virgin
olive oil

1 onion, sliced

5 garlic cloves, sliced

80ml (2fl oz) Cognac

1 red pepper,
deseeded and sliced

2 medium tomatoes,
skinned and sliced

1 tbsp tomato purée

1 pared strip of orange
peel

sprig of thyme

1 bay leaf

2 'petals' of star anise

180ml (6fl oz) dry
white wine

600ml (1 pint) good-
quality chicken stock

250g (9oz) small,
evenly sized waxy
potatoes, peeled and
quartered lengthways

5 tbsp rouille
(see page 7)

to serve

2 tbsp freshly chopped
flat-leaf parsley

slices of pain rustique
(rustic white bread)

Bouillabaisse

I've used fillets of fish, because finding small inshore fish could be difficult.

Serves 8

2 x 500g (1lb) cooked
lobsters

4 x 175–200g (6–7oz)
monkfish tails, skinned
and filleted

4 x 250–300g (9–11oz)
gurnard and John Dory fillets

150ml (¼ pint) olive oil

1 medium onion, chopped

1 leek, sliced

3 medium carrots, finely
chopped

½ small fennel head, finely
chopped

pinch of crushed dried
chillies

1 kg (2lb) conger eel or
pollack, skinned and cut
into chunks

50g (2oz) tomato purée

100ml (3½ fl oz) dry white
wine

2 litres (3½ pints) good
quality fish stock

a bouquet garni made from
thyme sprigs, bay leaves
and parsley stalks

4 garlic cloves, chopped

½ tsp saffron strands

½ tsp mild curry powder

a pinch of cayenne pepper

to serve

100g (4oz) rouille and
croutons (see page 7)

25g (1oz) Parmesan

450g (1lb) small potatoes

Step one Break off the legs and claws of the lobsters. Crack the shells of the claws with the back of a knife and break at the joints into smaller pieces. Cut the rest of the lobster in half lengthways, detach the head from the tail and cut each tailpiece across into three evenly sized pieces. Put the fish fillets and lobster pieces onto a tray, cover with clingfilm and keep chilled.

Step two Heat the oil in a large pan. Add the vegetables and crushed dried chillies and cook gently for 20 minutes until soft but not coloured. Add the conger eel or pollack and fry briskly with the vegetables for 3–4 minutes. Add the tomato purée, white wine and fish stock. Bring to the boil, add the bouquet garni, garlic, saffron, curry powder and a pinch of cayenne pepper and leave to simmer very gently, uncovered, for 1 hour. Meanwhile, make the rouille and the croûtons (see page 7).

Step three Preheat the oven to 150°C/300°F/gas 2. Pass the soup through a sieve into a pan, pressing as much of the liquid through the sieve as you can. Return the soup to a wide-based, shallow, clean pan, season to taste with salt, pepper and cayenne pepper, and bring back to a simmer. Add the monkfish fillets and cook for 1 minute. Then add the gurnard and John Dory fillets and the pieces of lobster, making sure that they are fully submerged in the soup. Simmer for 2 minutes. The fish will still be slightly undercooked at this point.

Step four Carefully lift the fish fillets and lobster pieces out of the soup onto a warmed serving plate, ladle over a small amount of the soup, cover with foil and put in the oven to keep warm, but don't leave for any more than 10 minutes. Ladle the soup into warmed soup plates and serve with the croûtons, rouille and grated Parmesan, and some small potatoes cooked in the soup, if you wish.

Poached Salmon with Cucumber and Dill Salad

The salmon is so much better when it is slightly undercooked, so I've given very precise instructions here. It goes without saying that the salmon should be of the highest quality, wild or organically farmed, and perfectly fresh.

Step one To make the court-bouillon, put all the ingredients into a pan and bring to the boil. Leave to simmer for 10 minutes and then strain into a deep roasting tin in which the fish fillet will fit. Place directly over the heat, bring up to the boil and then slide in the salmon, skin side up. Bring back to a simmer, simmer for just 1 minute and then turn off the heat and leave the fish to poach in the cooling liquid.

Step two By the time the liquid has cooled down the fish will be cooked – it should register about 50°C/120°F at the centre of the thickest part. Carefully lift the fish out, drain away the excess liquid and then place on an oval serving plate. Peel away the skin and then cover the fish with clingfilm. Keep it cool, but do not chill it.

Step three For the salad, peel the cucumbers and cut them into thin slices. Place a layer of the cucumber slices in a shallow dish and sprinkle with a little of the vinegar, chopped dill, sugar and salt. Continue to layer up the cucumber slices in the same way until all the ingredients have been used up. Cover and chill until ready to serve the salmon.

Serves 8

1kg (2lb 4oz) salmon fillet

for the court-bouillon

3 litres (5¼ pints) water

100g (4oz) fennel head, sliced

1 onion, sliced

3 bay leaves

1 tsp black peppercorns

300ml (½ pint) white wine

1 tbsp salt

for the salad

2 cucumbers

4 tbsp white wine vinegar

2 tbsp freshly chopped dill

1 tbsp caster sugar

½ tsp salt

Grilled Cod on Pommes Sarladaises with Truffle Oil

The combination of tomato and capers, the Sarladaise potatoes and the cod with a bit of bite to it is my idea of good bistro fish cooking.

Serves 4

4 x 175–225g (6–8 oz) pieces of thick unskinned cod fillet

15g (½ oz) melted butter, for brushing

for the sarladaise

1 kg (2 lb 4 oz) floury potatoes

4 heaped tbsp goose or duck fat

3 garlic cloves, chopped

25g (1 oz) freshly chopped flat-leaf parsley

1 tsp truffle oil

for the salad

6 medium-sized vine-ripened tomatoes, thinly sliced

1 small red onion, halved and thinly sliced

2 tsp nonpareilles capers, drained and rinsed

1 tsp red wine vinegar

pinch of caster sugar

4 tsp extra-virgin olive oil

1 tbsp freshly chopped flat-leaf parsley

Step one For the Sarladaise potatoes, peel and thickly slice the potatoes (about 5mm/¼ in thick). Heat 3 tablespoons of the fat in a large non-stick frying pan. Add the potatoes and some seasoning and fry over a medium heat for about 5 minutes until the bottom layer of potatoes is golden. Then turn the potatoes over and leave until another bottom layer is golden. Some of the potatoes will remain unbrowned, and as they cook the slices start to break up a little, but don't worry, this is how they should be. Repeat this for 15 minutes, making sure not to turn the potatoes before the bottom layer has browned. Then turn the heat down, cover and leave to cook very gently for a further 10 minutes.

Step two Mix the garlic and half the parsley leaves together to make a persillade. Uncover the potatoes and mix in the persillade and the truffle oil. Cover and leave to cook for 10 minutes, until the potatoes are tender when pierced with the tip of a knife.

Step three Meanwhile, brush the cod on both sides with the melted butter and season. Put skin-side up onto a baking sheet and grill for 8–10 minutes until cooked through.

Step four For the salad, arrange the sliced tomatoes in a shallow serving dish and scatter over the sliced red onion and the capers. Whisk together the red wine vinegar, sugar and a pinch of salt and pepper and then gradually whisk in the olive oil. Drizzle over the salad, scatter with parsley and set to one side.

Step five Uncover the pan of potatoes, turn up the heat and add the last tablespoon of fat. Fry for 2–3 minutes until the bottom layer is crisp and brown, then add the remaining chopped parsley and turn over briefly. To serve, spoon the potatoes onto 4 warm plates and rest the cod on top. Serve with the salad.

Sole Véronique

There's a nice story attached to the naming of this classic French dish. The chef-saucier of the Ritz in Paris, Monsieur Malley, left work after a busy lunch having instructed a young commis chef to add some tiny green Muscat grapes to the sole with white-wine sauce that was to be served that evening. On his return for service he discovered the young chef in a state of excitement; his young wife had just given birth to their first child, Véronique, and Monsieur Malley named the dish after her.

Step one To make the fleurons, preheat the oven to 200°C/400°F/ gas 6. Roll the pastry out thinly on a lightly floured surface and cut out eight 7½cm (3in) discs using a pastry cutter. Then, using the pastry cutter again, cut away one side of each disc to make a crescent-moon shape. Put onto a greased baking sheet and chill for 20 minutes. Then brush with beaten egg and with the tip of a small, sharp knife, lightly score a criss-cross pattern on each one. Bake for 20 minutes, or until puffed up and golden. Remove and keep warm. Reduce the oven temperature to 180°C/350°F/ gas 4.

Step two Season the sole fillets lightly on both sides, then fold them in half, skinned side innermost, and place side by side in a buttered shallow ovenproof dish. Pour over the stock, cover with foil and bake for 20 minutes.

Step three Remove the fish from the dish and put on a warmed serving plate. Cover with foil and keep warm. Pour the cooking liquor into a pan, add the vermouth, then bring to the boil and boil vigorously until reduced to about 6 tablespoons. Add the cream and a squeeze of lemon juice and simmer until it has thickened to a coating consistency.

Step four Add the grapes to the sauce and warm through gently. Season the sauce to taste, pour it over the fish and garnish with the puff pastry fleurons. Serve immediately.

Serves 4

8 x 75g (3oz) Dover sole fillets, skinned

600ml (1 pint) good-quality fish stock or chicken stock

85ml (3fl oz) dry vermouth, such as Noilly Prat

300ml (½ pint) double cream

a squeeze of fresh lemon juice

25–30 seedless green grapes, preferably Muscat, halved

for the fleurons garnish

250g (9oz) puff pastry

a little flour, for rolling out

a little beaten egg, for glazing

Fillets of John Dory with Olives, Capers and Rosemary

This dish is the same sort of assembly as a salad Niçoise if, like me, you use warm potatoes in it. It's very much a restaurant dish, where the success is largely based on the quality of the ingredients, the preciseness of the cooking of the fish and, perhaps most importantly, the attractive way the ingredients are put on the plate.

Serves 4

2 x 350–450g (12oz–1lb) John Dory, filleted

50ml (2fl oz) extra-virgin olive oil

4 small, waxy, new potatoes

2 anchovy fillets in olive oil, drained

3 pieces sun-dried tomato in olive oil, drained

a small handful of freshly chopped flat leaf parsley

4 very small, vine-ripened tomatoes, skinned, quartered and deseeded

8 black olives, pitted and cut in half

12 nonpareille capers

leaves from 1 x 5cm (2in) rosemary sprig

Step one Preheat the grill to high. Cut each John Dory fillet diagonally across into two similar-sized pieces. Brush each piece with olive oil, season with salt and pepper and place, skin side up, on a baking sheet. Cut each potato lengthways into quarters and cook in a pan of boiling, salted water for a few minutes until tender. Drain, return to the pan, cover and keep warm.

Step two Cut the anchovy fillets lengthways into fine slivers. Cut each piece of sun-dried tomato into thin strips. Very roughly chop the flat-leaf parsley, so that the leaves are still almost intact.

Step three Grill the John Dory fillets for 3–4 minutes until only just cooked. Meanwhile, put the remaining olive oil, potatoes, anchovies, sun-dried tomatoes, parsley, tomatoes, olives, capers and rosemary into a small, shallow pan and warm through over a low heat, but do not overheat the oil. Then season and very gently stir the ingredients around so that they are all coated in the oil and parsley.

Step four Overlap two pieces of John Dory onto four warmed plates and divide the contents of the pan over the fish, making it look as attractive as possible. Serve immediately.

Roasted Salmon on Roasted Tomatoes with Salsa Verde

To make life easy, prepare the salmon in the morning and chill, but remove it from the fridge 30 minutes before roasting to allow it to come back to room temperature.

Step one Preheat the oven to 220°C/425°F/gas 7. Chop together the parsley and mint leaves, 3 tablespoons of the capers, the anchovy fillets and 1 garlic clove on a board into a coarse paste and season to taste with a little salt.

Step two Line the base of a large baking sheet or roasting tin with a sheet of non-stick baking paper and then lay the tomato slices in rows of four down the centre (diagonally if necessary, so that your salmon will fit). Scatter over the rest of the capers, the remaining garlic, cut into slices, half the chilli flakes and the leaves of all but one sprig of the thyme, and sprinkle over 3 tablespoons of the oil, the water and some salt. This will prevent the salmon from sticking and produce a lovely sauce to serve with the fish.

Step three Brush the skin side of one salmon fillet with a little of the remaining oil, season lightly and place skin side down on top of the tomatoes, then cover with the salsa verde mixture. Place the second salmon fillet up on top. Brush the skin with the rest of the oil and scatter with chilli flakes and the leaves from the remaining thyme sprig. Season with salt and pepper.

Step four Roast the fish for 25 minutes, until the skin is lightly browned and the flesh still slightly pink in the centre. Remove the salmon and leave it to rest briefly.

Step five To serve, cut the salmon into portions and serve with some thyme-flavoured tomatoes and a little of the cooking juices. Accompany with steamed new potatoes and green beans.

Serves 10–12

2.5–2.75kg (5½–6lb) salmon, scaled and filleted or 2 x 1kg (2¼lb) salmon fillets

for the tomatoes and salsa verde

1 big bunch flat-leaf parsley leaves

a handful of mint leaves

4 tbsp capers

6 anchovy fillets in olive oil, drained

3 garlic cloves

4 large, vine-ripened tomatoes, each cut into 4 slices

½ tsp dried chilli flakes

a large bunch of thyme

about 4 tbsp olive oil

10 tbsp water

For a video masterclass on filleting salmon, go to
www.mykitchentable.co.uk/videos/basting

203

Grilled Red Snapper with Portobello Mushrooms and Spinach

I'm afraid that this recipe is a little wasteful, but the Japanese would use the trimmings from the fish and mushrooms for another dish, such as fishcakes.

Serves 4

450g (1lb) piece of red snapper fillet, taken from a fish weighing about 2–2.25kg (4½–5lb)

4 large portobello mushrooms, cleaned and trimmed but stalks left in place

sunflower oil, for brushing

200ml (7fl oz) dashi (see page 80)

100g (4oz) English spinach, washed and well drained

a few drops of dark soy sauce

finely grated lemon zest, to garnish

for the dipping sauce

3 tbsp dashi (see page 80)

3 tbsp mirin (Japanese rice wine)

3 tbsp light soy sauce

Step one Soak eight 18cm (7in) bamboo skewers in some cold water for 30 minutes. Preheat the grill to high. Mix together the ingredients for the dipping sauce and set aside.

Step two Trim the belly flap away from the fillet of fish and trim the remaining loin very neatly, so that you have one long, evenly shaped piece of fish. Cut it across into eight 40g (1½oz) pieces, about 2cm (¾in) thick. Slice each mushroom through the stalk into slices about 5mm (¼in) thick – you should get three perfect slices from each mushroom. Discard the remainder.

Step three Working with two slices of fish at a time, lay them flat on a board and thread them through the skin, onto two parallel skewers. Brush them on both sides with oil, season generously with salt and lay on the rack of a grill pan. Put the mushroom slices on a lightly oiled baking sheet and sprinkle with salt. Grill the fish for 2 minutes on each side and the mushrooms for 1 minute only.

Step four Bring the dashi to the boil in a small pan. Add the spinach and, as soon as it has wilted into the stock, drain well and season lightly with salt.

Step five Lift two of the skewers onto each of four warmed plates and overlap three of the mushroom slices alongside. Add a small pile of spinach to each plate, sprinkle a few drops of dark soy sauce onto the mushrooms and scatter the fish with a little of the lemon zest. Serve immediately, with the dipping sauce.

10 9 8 7 6 5 4 3 2 1

Published in 2011 by BBC Books,
an imprint of Ebury Publishing.
A Random House Group company

Recipes © Rick Stein 2011

Book design © Woodlands Books Ltd 2011

All recipes contained in this book first appeared in
Rick Stein's *Seafood* (2001), *French Odyssey* (2005),
Mediterranean Escapes (2007), *Coast to Coast* (2008)
and *Far Eastern Odyssey* (2009).

Rick Stein has asserted his right to be identified as the
author of this Work in accordance with the Copyright,
Designs and Patents Act 1988

The Random House Group Limited
Reg. No. 954009

Addresses for companies within the Random House
Group can be found at www.randomhouse.co.uk

A CIP catalogue record for this book is available from the
British Library

The Random House Group Limited supports The Forest
Stewardship Council (FSC), the leading international forest certification organization. All our titles that are printed
on Greenpeace approved FSC certified paper carry the
FSC logo. Our paper procurement policy can be found at
www.rbooks.co.uk/environment

To buy books by your favourite authors and register for
offers visit www.rbooks.co.uk

Printed and bound in the UK by Butler, Tanner and
Dennis Ltd
Colour origination by AltaImage

Commissioning Editor: Muna Reyal
Project Editor: Laura Higginson
Designer: Lucy Stephens
Photographer: William Reavell © Woodlands Books
Ltd 2011 (see also credits below)
Food Stylist: Annie Rigg and Denise Smart
Props Stylist: Liz Belton
Copy-editor: Anna Hitchin
Production: Helen Everson

Photography on page 4 by James Murphy © Woodlands
Books Ltd; pages 12, 14, 22, 29, 33, 37, 38, 41, 42, 49, 54,
58, 61, 62, 65, 70, 73, 74, 82, 85, 86, 88, 94, 96, 98, 105,
108, 114, 117, 121, 133, 135, 141, 151, 157, 158, 161, 165,
166, 173, 174, 181, 182, 185, 186, 190, 192, 197 © James
Murphy, 9, 17, 18, 25, 50, 78, 90, 93, 122, 125, 127, 129,
130, 138, 149, 177 © Earl Carter.

ISBN: 978 1 849 90158 1